CLASSIC CAR MUSEUM GUIDE

MOTOR CARS, MOTORCYCLES AND MACHINERY

LANCE COLE

'From Amilcar to Austin, from BSA to Vincent, from AEC to
Scammell, via Rover, Triumph, and all points in between, notably
interrupted by the name British Leyland, our museums are
populated with wonderful memories in metal. Major museums and
minor museums make up the museum body that is at the soul of our
enthusiasm and worship for the cars and motorcycles of the past.'

PEN & SWORD
TRANSPORT

AN IMPRINT OF PEN & SWORD BOOKS LTD.
YORKSHIRE – PHILADELPHIA

First published in Great Britain in 2020 by
Pen and Sword Transport
An imprint of
Pen & Sword Books Ltd
Yorkshire - Philadelphia

Copyright © Lance Cole, 2020

ISBN 978 1 52673 587 4

The right of Lance Cole to be identified as Author of this work has been asserted by him
in accordance with the Copyright, Designs and Patents Act 1988.

A CIP catalogue record for this book is available from the British Library.

All rights reserved. No part of this book may be reproduced or transmitted in any form
or by any means, electronic or mechanical including photocopying, recording or by
any information storage and retrieval system, without permission from the Publisher in
writing.

Typeset in Sabon LT Std 11/14
by Aura Technology and Software Services, India.

Printed and bound in India by Replika Press Pvt. Ltd.

Pen & Sword Books Ltd incorporates the Imprints of Pen & Sword Books Archaeology,
Atlas, Aviation, Battleground, Discovery, Family History, History, Maritime, Military,
Naval, Politics, Railways, Select, Transport, True Crime, Fiction, Frontline Books, Leo
Cooper, Praetorian Press, Seaforth Publishing, Wharncliffe and White Owl.

For a complete list of Pen & Sword titles please contact

PEN & SWORD BOOKS LIMITED
47 Church Street, Barnsley, South Yorkshire, S70 2AS, England
E-mail: enquiries@pen-and-sword.co.uk
Website: www.pen-and-sword.co.uk

Or

PEN AND SWORD BOOKS
1950 Lawrence Rd, Havertown, PA 19083, USA
E-mail: Uspen-and-sword@casematepublishers.com
Website: www.penandswordbooks.com

CONTENTS

ACKNOWLEDGEMENTS

Specific thanks to the Atwell-Wilson Motor Museum, Bicester Heritage, the British Motor Museum, Bugatti Trust, Haynes International, the Lakeland Museum, National Motorcycle Museum, National Motor Museum Trust, the Shuttleworth Collection and the Australasian Motor Museums Association. Thanks and acknowledgements to all the museums who assisted with content listings and photography and offered proper tea and homemade cake – all paid for! Acknowledgements to staffers at *Classic and Sports Car*, *Practical Classics*, and *Classic Cars* for verbal opinions. Thanks to Alan Ward – classic tractor and classic car fettler, engineer, and friend. A salute to Alex Rankin my old Saab mate, Robin Morley for the same and also to James Walshe for his kindness and enthusiasm. Likewise to Richard Gunn. A salute also to Tom Donney and his Saabs in the USA. Thanks are due to my Citroën DS-owning grandfather Tom, and to my car enthusiast father Francis. And for her patience and support, thanks are due my wife Anna, who tolerates the memorabilia and the wallowing in nostalgia.

Photographic Notes: Unless stated otherwise, all photographs are by the author. Please note: The author Lance F. Cole has no connection to 'Lance Cole Photography' or such named website or entity.

INTRODUCTION

J-P Wimille's Bugatti T59/50B on the start line at Prescott when it arrived for display at the Bugatti Trust Museum, returning to Prescott after eight decades.

Motor cars, motorcycles & memorabilia:
A tale of pursuing petroliana, nostalgia being better than it used to be...

The magic of man's motoring has now lasted well over 100 years, which means that preserving and celebrating the past and all that has passed under our wheels, suddenly seems even more important. The motor car or automobile shaped the twentieth century. Today, in the first decades of the twenty-first century, preserving that period and celebrating the concept of the car museum seems suddenly very relevant to the motoring enthusiast. Car clubs and car museums are busier than they ever have been. There is a reason why. Put simply, nostalgia is big business and very popular.

Less than 50 years ago, the number of commercially established automotive or 'motoring' museums in Great Britain could be counted on one hand. In Europe, less than 30 existed. America had many 'invisible' small motoring museums or personal collections. Some still exist, yet multi-million pound museums now offer something new. The rise of the private museum is also noteworthy. Large, glossy museums with money are indeed good, but we should never forget the sheer authenticity of the smaller, older, or hidden gems of the provincial museums – nor the commitment of the people that run them. 'Off the radar' of museum consciousness some may be, but they are true hidden gems.

Today, the motoring museum business is big business and many museums exist, over 150 in Europe alone and hundreds worldwide. So nostalgia may very well be better than it used to be. To prove the point, Vauxhall have expanded their Vauxhall Heritage Centre in Luton and are opening up their collection to the public on a more frequent basis. In Derbyshire, a company called the Great British Car Journey, is to open a major new classic car museum at the former Johnson & Nephew Wire Works. The project is to be called the Ambergate Motor Heritage Centre and at the time of writing was well advanced in its plans.

I wrote this book as part of an odyssey taking in some of the world's finest driving roads and as many museums, large and small, that I could visit en route. From the outback of Australia, to the roads of rural France, across America, through Africa, and deep into Europe, this has been a true adventure of automobilia amid a petroliania persuasion. Here is my museum odyssey that really ought to be a television adventure hosted by this Cole – not Henry Cole despite his 'sheds' brilliance.

I tried to keep my ego in my backpack and listen to the stories of the cars, motorcycles, tractors, and strange, spluttering devices and their owners. Only the occasional imbecile was encountered – why is that the donning of a hi-vis jacket sometimes results in the lowering of brain function?

Nothing is definitive of course, but this is my stab at a motoring enthusiasts guide to our memorabilia and noteworthy museum pieces. The selection is entirely personal, taken from my own visits and those of others. Any omissions are either

accidental or circumstantial. No agenda and no funding nor sponsorship, not a single free ticket, lies within the book or its selection. I paid my own way.

What became obvious on that road-trip – meeting so many wonderful characters and enthusiasts – is that we love our cars as much now as we did in the past, but in a new way. Indeed, according to a recent report by the Federation of British Historic Vehicle Clubs, forty eight per cent of the British population think that historic vehicles (built prior to 1985) should be preserved for the future. Such is our love of old cars, such is the importance of securing the museums that house, display, and restore them. Driving our old cars is vital and many museums ensure that their exhibits actually work. Bodies like British Motor Heritage and numerous owners clubs and societies inhabit the great hinterland of old car enthusiasm that now represents a major social and historical movement.

Old vehicles, old motorcycles, old artefacts, and the museums that house so many of them, really are in a new era of their greatest ever profile and interest.

In 2019, official figures showed that more people were visiting museums in Great Britain than ever before. Libraries might be in crisis, but museums are booming. Yet sadly there have been some museum closures due to various reasons. Doune Motor Museum, the Donington Collection, 'Cars of the Stars', 'Automobilia', the Johns/Exmoor Classic Collection, the Nigel Mansell Collection, the Stondon Motor Museum, and the Bournemouth Transport Museum, are just some of the museum names that have gone in recent years – sadly roped off for the final time.

Many car manufacturers have either exceeded their century, others are approaching it. Some of our museums have been around a long time too. Incredibly, some car makers are selling off their own in-house museum exhibits and heritage collections; Citroën recently divested itself of some if its vital historical vehicles from its own conservatoire museum. The Bertone collection has also been disbanded. Nigel Mansell has closed his motorsport museum. Some of our older and long-established European museums have also had to close. A huge and crucial loss to motorsport history also being the closure of the Donington/Wheatcroft museum. Yet museums set in sheds and barns, and those housed in multi-million dollar architectural landmarks, continue to offer us something old amid the new age of the museum. Fiat's new FCA heritage museum in its old Mirafiori base Turin is a true shrine to all things four-wheeled that have stemmed from northern Italy. 15,000sqm of hub has been created.

The origins of museums – specifically motoring museums or transport museums – are that they are created either through national scientific or academic requirements, or through the ideology of a corporate marque, or, as in so many cases, the personal enthusiasm and commitment of one man or woman or a family, in to a collection that becomes a museum. We might suggest that it is the personal collections, self-funded at start-up, that still provide us with the core of the global motoring and transport enthusiast museum sector.

When was the first car or motor museum established? Surely it was at Beaulieu in the 1950s. However, there is plenty of evidence that private car collections as de facto museum-type collections are recorded as far back as the Edwardian era, but the First World War seems to have put paid to such indulgences in an age when the motor car was for the rich and the carnage of that war left so many scars. Beaulieu (as the National Motor Museum) remains Britain's founding father of the motor museum, but much has changed – as Beaulieu has had to itself.

Today, there are very few 'bad' museums and many 'good' ones: a whole new world of motor museums that have become updated, expanded, invigorated, now exists in Britain and beyond. From major national museum landmarks to private collections and smaller, provincial affairs, this book guides the reader through what is on offer to the dedicated enthusiast and to the more casual visitor. Cars, buses, lorries, motorcycles, steam vehicles, and motorsport icons, all are included.

Despite the internet of things and its immediate access, maybe the reality of a book that collates everything together and offers us an all-in-one guide around our motoring museums and their contents, is a good idea in an age of digital quick reference and click bait gratification. A motor museum companion was my intention; the glossary of old car terms should provide assistance to the non-expert reader and refresh know-it-alls from their torpor.

In the new age of the museum, our motor museums have, for want of a better word, become 'shrines' to our automobilia or even what some might call automania. New displays, new techniques, and new thinking frame the true 'new' age of the museum. Like nostalgia, museums are better than they used to be. We even have an 'international museums day' which is surely an excuse to drive your classic car to a museum, or ride your motorcycle to one.

The trend to put everything behind glass or plastic and separate it from visitors is less obvious in motor museums and we must be thankful for that. Roped-off cars are inevitable to avoid damage, but many smaller 'survivor' museums have re-invented their displays to become more engaging. Digital screens and interactive kit are *not* essential! The key is to remain authentic; if it can crack that, a motoring museum will prosper.

Entranced by enamel, pursuing petroliana

Museums are also packed with wonderful automobilia, vintage-era artefacts and petroliana such as petrol pumps and their globes, enamel signs, cans, badges, advertising, brochures, pamphlets and mascots to name just a few of the things that now seem like lost treasures. Indeed a dedicated sub-culture of ephemera, artefacts, books, and memorabilia now exists and some achieve huge prices. Recently, a vintage petrol pump-globe collection sold for over £100,000 with

Richard Edmonds Auctions, who claim to be Europe's leading auctioneers of automobilia and petroliana.

The great era of automobilia and of enamelled signage seems now to be a lost world of loveliness to which many of us have become addicted. Signage is special stuff. People buy it, all over the world. Enamelled items along with auto-artefacts are a huge lure, and big business. Petrol pumps, cans, mascots, cabinets, cases, pumps, you think of it and an entire sub-culture of motoring memorabilia emerges.

The excellent 'Petroliana' web site run by Alan Chandler (and publications) is one of the first to try and do justice to the amazing world of the old stuff of petroleum, and of 'enamelism' (or enamellism) as I prefer to call it, for it is an excellent 'ism' to worship.

Vintage Motoring-UK are well known collectors and retailers of vintage memorabilia, and enamel signs and petroliana artefacts are their thing; visits to their collection and retail premises in Leicestershire need to be arranged (generally open from Wednesday to Sunday but check before going). Rob Arnold's Automobilia-UK is also open to visitors/buyers by appointment and can be found in Derbyshire. Tramps of Nottinghamshire has also supplied automobilia for well over a decade. Other memorabilia suppliers exist, including Special Auction Services at Newbury whose 'road-show' are great.

On an international stage, try iTrouvaille (itrouvaille.com) for one of the glossiest of automobilia services. Trouve-to-trouvaille, stems from the French for 'find' and finds are what 'i ' (I for internet) trouvaille is all about, in a truly upmarket manner. This is automobile artefacts taken to the exquisite. Rural France remains packed with old stuff seeking a discoverer; truffle hunters still search.

Bonhams are perhaps the apogee of the automotive auction world, and yes, they too have embraced automobilia and petroliana. But don't forget automobilia auction houses like H and H, and Hansons of Derbyshire, or Dominic Winter of Wiltshire, the well-known Richard Edmonds (also of Wiltshire), amid a network of provincial auctions that feed the great automobilia movement. Motorsport fans are also well catered for in this field and online via excellent portals such as motoring-man/GP Box. London boasts the brilliant Pullman Gallery/Collection/Studio of automobilia, an emporium that is a very serious 'shrine' indeed – take lots of money!

Many of our museums contain collections of pumps, signage, enamel, and petrol-related artefacts. Indeed, we are beginning to see specific displays of such items and they are to be encouraged and not to be missed. Old signs are magic. Chipped enamel is a drug, a collector's true 'buzz'. No museum worth its salt should ignore this wonderful world of automobilia. Sadly, one of the world's first dedicated petroliana museums has had to close due to the death of its owner. Collector Jeff Pedersen created his 'General Petroleum Museum' collection at Pine

Street in Seattle, USA, in the 1980s and 1990s. It may have been the first true, solely petroliana museum.

In Britain today, the largest collection of automobilia may be at the superb Lakeland Museum and provides another reason to spend a day there.

All over the world, cars are collected, but so too are items of automobilia and petroliana. This is a massive culture, a huge movement with many rooms and attics of delight to discover.

Petroliana truly is a sound from another room.

Somehow, amid all these motoring themes, we have to persuade today's youth, many of who have little idea of what a pre-1990s, non-digital car is, to take an interest in old cars, 'proper' mechanically operated cars. To do so, new techniques are needed, hence the new age of the motoring museum amid a new thinking.

Some readers might prefer the shiny halls and cars of the Petersen in California, or the Mullin Museum, or the essential exhibits of the National Motor Museum, British Motor Museum, or Haynes International. Vital as these leaders are, we should not ignore the smaller museums that are by no means 'lesser', they are just different.

Indeed, certain readers might prefer the smaller, more intimate exhibition spaces of provincial gems such as the Lakeland Museum, Filchings, Anglesey, the Murray Motorcycle Museum, the Sammy Miller Museum, to cite just a few British examples, but sadly the London Motorcycle Museum has just been closed permanently, a big loss.

Amongst such names, the Matthewson family run the North Yorkshire Motor Museum at their garage in Thornton-Le-Dale and it thrives as a gem that also restores, sells and exhibits cars and motorcycles in an authentic manner amid an auction-house setting. This is the way to make collecting classic cars pay. They know about Jowett of Yorkshire and Gerald Palmer's styling too.

Visit England has created a 'Hidden Gems' award for smaller, lesser known museums and this underlines how vital the smaller museum and its culture is.

Rodger Dudding's Studio434 in London is another (but different) new hub concept that delivers an amazing car collection amid a commercial reality.

Across America, Australia, and Europe, a whole collage of differing contexts of the motor museum exist.

The Classic Remise (Dusseldorf and Berlin) is another new classic car 'hub' concept that reinvents the context of the museum in a new context so different from a provincial private collection.

One of the best European museums I have visited is the Two-Wheels and NSU Museum (*Deutsches Zweirad und NSU Museum*) at Neckarsulm. There, in a medieval building, including in caves, lies the full story of NSU cars and motorcycles in a modern yet truly authentic museum setting and story – it is just brilliant. And it is *not* an architect-designed, 'statement' building packed with

digital extravagance and glazed-in exhibits, nor is it populated by expensively dressed haughty 'attendants' who make you feel insignificant as a few, a very few, museums can on occasion, sadly achieve.

If you are in Barbados (as so many Brits are) you cannot miss the Mallalieu Motor Collection at Hastings, Bridgetown. The owner, Allard-fancier Bill Mallalieu is always on hand to chat about cars too, amid relaxed surroundings – with a drink!

Museum Angkut, Batu City, Indonesia? A superb motoring museum stuffed with cars and motorcycles in Batu City Indonesia! To coin a current phrase, who knew? Well worth the visit if you just happen to in the area. What of the HeriTran Classic Car Museum in Hanoi – another surprise amid Vietnam's tragic but fascinating history – easily accessible via Vietnam Airways and their fantastic Premium Economy cabin on a direct service from London.

As in America, Australia hosts a number of small, personal collection-based museums that lie beyond the larger halls of museum fame. A visit to 'Charlies' at Arthur's Seat in Victoria, will provide a very real experience of the personal collection angle to a motoring museum and emporium of motoring paraphernalia. The man even has a Tatra! Over in West Australia, the York Museum is fantastic (it boasts an Allard): the West Coast Motor Museum has 180 cars on show in its superb setting – with 1,500 scale models. Other really good museums populate W.A., and the other Australian States, notably Victoria, and a quick reference guide to them is included in this book.

Of interest, Australia operated a restricted car body import scheme in the inter-war years. This meant that for every fully-bodied, finished car allowed into Australia, two bare chassis (requiring bodies) were allowed in under a 'two-for-one' rule. This gave rise to expansion in local, Australian coachbuilding, notably in Melbourne, Sydney, and Perth. Today it means that some very rare Australian-bodied old cars can be seen in Australian museums and overseas. There is even talk of Australian-bodied Bugattis being built near Sydney.

Beyond Australia, can anyone really argue that Franschhoek Motor Museum in South Africa is anything other than utterly superb to the point of being world class. In South America, Argentina (which boasted an often forgotten car-industry and motorsport golden era), Brazil, Chile, Peru, Uruguay, and Mexico all boast car museums. Alfa-Romeo, Saab, and BMW cars were all built from CKD kits in Argentina – many such oldies still thrive. Argentina has a strong motorsport history beyond the Fangio legend; Erik Carlsson rallied Saabs there and I was stunned to see old Saab 93-96 cars trundling around Buenos Aires.

Chile has *five* motor museums – now there was a surprise. The roads of Paraguay are still classic car treasure troves and a private motoring museum is due to be opened in Paraguay. Many small, private collections dating back to the 1920s are also secreted away in Chile – as they are in Zimbabwe and Kenya.

Brooklands action. Museum piece on the move as intended.

Bicester is brilliant

A fine example of the new life that motoring memorabilia and wider automotive passion now inhabits can be seen at Bicester Heritage. Daniel Geoghegan is the man who began this lateral thinking reinvention as a modern 'hub' encapsulating so many aspects of our motoring enthusiasm. Bicester's 'Scramble' days represent an active, moving museum that takes in businesses, restorers, curatorial guardians, owners, car clubs and the classic car public in a unique and brilliant way. Significant things are planned for Bicester in the next five years as part of Bicester Motion. Just add more enamel and petroleum artefacts, please.

What of commercial vehicles, and agricultural devices? They have their shrines too. Vintage tractors, lorries and buses – all have their homes.

Small museums are great, gems that should not be eclipsed by the glamour of the multi-million pound museum. The sheer authenticity of places like Atwell-Wilson, Flichings, the North Yorkshire Motor Museum, the Oxford Bus and Morris Motors Museum, Murray's Motorcycle Museum or Sammy Millers collection, must be supported. The Bugatti Trust's museum is small but of the highest quality and cannot be underestimated in its importance to the motoring enthusiast nor as educational resource for future engineers and designers.

Further afield, what of the evocative and superb Loheac Museum of the Manoir, in Brittany? This is a one of Europe's top motoring museums, yet wonderfully rural.

What of Porsche's multi-million shrine of a museum at Zuffenhausen Stuttgart? The Henry Ford Museum in Detroit? These are all different but all brilliant.

Suddenly our museums are something new and more dynamic, a true new chapter in in the history of the motor museum.

The Nomenclature

Superfluity seems to sound like a word that goes with museum, along with, oil, two-stroke, crankshaft, coachbuilt, copper grease, flitch panel, roller-bearing, skiff, Scintilla, *sedanca de ville*, steam regulator, cycle car, *voiturette*, tumblehome, cabriolet and paraphernalia; such things amid the art of the museum visit must be interspersed with home-made 'real' chemical-free cake and, a pot of tea made with fully developed real tea leaves, or proper coffee ('instant' so-called coffee is not allowed), neither are 'tea' bags that dispense watered dust taken from the floor of a factory). Proper cars and real cake go well together.

From Amilcar to Austin, from BSA to Vincent, from AEC to Scammell, via Rover, Triumph, and all points in between, notably interrupted by the name British Leyland, our museums are populated with wonderful memories in metal. Major museums and minor museums make up the museum body that is at the soul of our enthusiasm and worship for the cars and motorcycles of the past.

But museums have to be viable and make money in order to preserve and persevere with that history.

Cars as pieces of engineering and industrial design are all that and more; they are works of art too. Like motorcycles, aircraft or boats and ships, the car is an inanimate object, a collection of metals, alloys, woods, plastics, materials and more, yet that somehow takes on a character, a true personality. Some may even perceive the psychometry of the original story of a car underneath its patina. Cars and most two, four, or multi-wheeled vehicles *are* true characters.

Museums are where the machines of our past, of several *belle epoch* eras can be seen and studied.

Motorsport

Motorsport still represents a pinnacle of the century of man's motoring. Museums of motorsport mean much and it is concerning to see the Donington Collection of such cars, and Mr B. Tom Wheatcroft's revered pieces (and notably his son's militaria), being closed as this is written. Opened in 1973, Donington contained the world's most significant collection of single-seater racing cars and was sited at Donington Park – the first true, solely dedicated and *permanent* road-racing circuit or course in England, despite an interpretation by the claims of others! But let's not forget Brooklands, and what of the 'grand prix' type race at Bexhill in 1902? Haynes International does motorsport proud, and so do to the motorcycle museums.

Incidentally, there was a Dodington Carriage Museum fifty plus miles west of Donington. Dodington housed a significant and much written-about horse-drawn

A great display. BMC/BL prototypes as exhibited at the superb British Motor Museum. (Photo: BMM)

carriage collection from the 1970s onwards and the occasional, confused and geographically challenged far eastern visitor may not have been unknown – as they looked for racing cars! However, Dodington Carriage Museum is now seemingly invisible.

Over 2.5 million people are said to have visited Donington; we are forced to ask what will happen to the Donington Collection/Wheatcroft exhibits? Will they reappear at a venue or in a new format after this book is published? Let us hope so. And yet it is suggested that they are to be sold off. To signify a point, the ex-Donington collection March 701/1 (Chris Amon's 'works' car as the first March Formula One car) has at the time of writing, been put up for sale through Taylor and Crawley of London. As it stands, Donington represents a huge omission from our story by dint of circumstance. After all, the collection contained everything from a BRM and ERA, to a Simca-Gordini, to a Maserati 8CM, the 1940s Cisitalia-Porsche, and on to 1970s Grand Prix and World Class cars and names such as Brabham, Lotus -Climax, McLaren-Ford, Cosworth, and many more gems of motorsport heritage. We can only hope that some form of reincarnation of the collection may be possible. Meanwhile, a wonderful new book *Donington Park: The Pioneers*, tells the tale of this circuit, its history, and the Wheatcroft achievements.

Yet was one of the reasons for Donington's failing being that it failed to modernise? But why should a lack of digital display condemn a museum? The harsh fact is that Donington was, in the main, much as it was in the 1970s. No bad thing you might say, but museums *have* moved on.

Motorsport remains a vital ingredient to our museums and is a theme that is beyond fashion or passing interest.

Speedsport at Silverstone offers a motorsport gallery and a 'live' workshop. Run by Mike O'Brien, Speedsport is not a museum, but it is one of those vital components in the world of cars and motorsport. The Speedsport gallery and sales point is inspired.

Motorsport fans cannot miss the *Conservatoire de la Monoplace*, Circuit Nevers Magny Cours. There, the history of French single-seat racing cars is well told amid the blue of a Ligier headline theme. Matra, Gordini, Bonnet, Martini, Renault, et al, all are superbly exhibited in a modern museum of true style.

Peter Mullin (of California museum and Bugatti fame) has plans for a major new Mullin Automotive Museum in West Oxfordshire in an 'Mullin Automotive Park' or museum which could create yet another shrine to the motor car and one with a twist. Houses and accommodation on-site will allow residents or visitors to display their cars as exhibits; a new take on museum status. The locals might object to more building, even if some of them live in new-build semi-rural, elitist housing estates themselves. And can the rural economy forego the new jobs Mullin's museum would create? And is not the locality packed with clogged main roads, jammed villages, 'rat-run' lanes, heavy traffic and engine-sourced air pollution anyway? What is a few more blinged-up Range Rovers amongst the ones that already live in the area with NIMBY plates? Why not add a bit more – after all such has not stopped expansion happening everywhere *else*, has it?

As this is written, Mullin's British emporium looks like being realised. How wonderful.

Dropping in at Aerospace Bristol and recalling Bristol Cars Ltd (in a museum supported by the Bristol Aerospace Collection and the Bristol Owners Heritage Trust), as well as seeing Concorde 'Alpha Fox' and, the Bristol Britannia – both as airliner and as a car – is a superb experience even if the cafe is not exactly cheap. Calling at the superb and ever-expanding Bicester Heritage centre (say hello to Historit), stopping off at the Bugatti Owners Club and the Bugatti Trust, visiting Beaulieu, Brooklands, Haynes, Filchings, The British Motor Museum, the Science Museum store at Wroughton and so many more, really has been huge fun. What of the £70million motoring memorial that is the Zaha Hadid-designed Riverside Museum of Transport in Glasgow? This stunning building and collection represent the recent heights of the museum movement, replacing the old Kelvin-Hall based Glasgow Transport museum.

A trip to the Isle of Man also reveals four transport museums; the superb Isle of Man Motor Museum of the Cunningham Collection now assumes international

status amid the 'names' of motor museums, yet is only six years old. Quite an achievement and a motorcyclists' heaven too. The long-standing Murray Motor museum provides motorcyclists with an interesting take on several themes.

The Design Museum in London should not be ignored either, for it too is a motor and mechanical shrine.

The Science Museum has decided to take a different route to displaying transport history and some car buffs do not find its choices ideal. Yet a visit to the Science Museum store at Wroughton is compelling and fascinating; there lies true treasure, yet mostly unseen and almost in secret.

Motorcyclists cannot but saviour and sup at the grail that is the National Motorcycle Museum – again the result of one man and his family's enthusiasm and efforts, and now also a superb, international grade exhibit and resource that also gets people involved – actually riding its machines on site.

Sometimes there is a gulf between the two tribes of motor car, and motor cycling enthusiasts, but there is no reason why there should be. But it's up to the reader to decide their personal choice.

Motors and Mustard

Various halts in France and beyond have provided much motoring joy. It is hard to leave somewhere like the wonderful Loheac motor museum in Brittany, or Michel Pont's gripping collection at the Château de Savigny-les-Beaune, which is also close to the home of the best mustard makers on the planet, Fallot and Company.

As for the simply brilliant Saab Museum in Trollhattan, it is beyond superb and was an early pointer to the new age of the museum 'culture' as we know it. The Vastergotland Museum in Sweden is also wonderful museum and one often given to automotive exhibitions. As for the Porsche Museum in Stuttgart, it is a cathedral of a shrine to Porsche. Germany is of course, crammed with motor museums of all varieties.

The Louwman Collection in the Netherlands reeks of niched quality and is a serious contender for the title of one of Europe's best, within its context that bizarrely includes Toyotas set alongside upper crust European marques at their most exquisite.

India has several transport museums that are full of classic cars from the colonial and post-colonial eras. Many rare and interesting cars can still be found in India. In fact, the assorted vintage car museums of India are very special and could form the basis of a car enthusiast's touring holiday. In Mumbai there is a bus museum at Anik bus depot.

If you get to Australia, you cannot miss the York Motor Museum near Perth Western Australia, nor miss the tale of red dust racers in the outback and the book that was written about them by Graeme Cocks. A quiet town York may be, but

Aussie motoring rules way out west, just as it does further east in Victoria and beyond where it is not all about Holden or Ford. The outback, by the way, is still full of old cars.

Victoria's historic motoring is celebrated at Geelong, and Phillip Island and should not be missed. There is also Bathurst and its circuit and museum just over the State border too. The Qantas Founders' Museum at Longreach, Queensland is about aircraft not cars, but cannot be missed if mechanicals are your thing. It is a simply brilliant and very real experience that is well worth the trip out from the coast. Reach it on Qantas of course – Q.A.N.T.A.S., the Queensland and Northern Territories Aerial Services, in case you did not know.

Across the Tasman Strait lies New Zealand and you should not miss the automotive and aviation activities at the National Transport and Toy Museum at Wanaka.

Cars and aircraft share a similar and closely linked heritage, especially circa 1905-1950; it is common for motoring museum to display aviation (or aeronautical) exhibits. After all, Bristol made aircraft before they made cars, as did Saab, Rumpler, Voisin. BMW also built aero-engines, Packard did likewise. Frederick Lanchester was an aerodynamics pioneer and went on to build advanced cars. The brilliant Bugattis of course designed and built cars, motorcycles, aircraft, trains and more.

We all have differing tastes and some of us are one-make fans, but many car enthusiasts are of a broader vision and dabble in cars that range from 1980s modern classics, back through post-1940s classic cars, and beyond into vintage and veteran era.

J-P Wimille's Bugatti T59/50B racer seen at Prescott for the first time in eight decades.

How can you argue with the genius of Phillip Vincent's engineering mind across his Black Shadow and Black Prince motorcycles? How many people know that Vincent invented and built a working jet-ski (the 'Amanda' water scooter) decades before such device became common place?

What of the Fordson Major, the Morris Minor van, Land Rover Series One, VW Beetle, Saab 96, and Yamaha 125, all being devices that I learned to drive and ride on as a child on our farm? These are my passions, and you will have yours, for we motoring fans are, it seems, touched by the cars of our childhood, the cars of our parents and grandparents, and the cars that we develop an affinity for – via reasons that only each one of us can understand.

Magazine moments

If we were all one-marque fanatics, classic car magazines would not sell because each issue contains a range of car makes and the stories of cars. I read more than one up-market classic car magazine every month. This may seem a touch esoteric, but I also read and devour the less highbrow, yet vital *Practical Classics* and *Classic Car Weekly* – not to mention regular sight of American and Australian magazines. *Classic and Sports Car* magazine's Martin Buckley has his own private collection of cars and memorabilia which is not open to the public, but what a shame his 'shed' does not (yet?) host an annual open day for enthusiasts of Lancia, or NSU, or eccentric persuasions of that ilk.

Then there are gems of portals like the *Vintagent*, and magazines of such glorious ilk as *Cafe Racer*, *Classic Motorcycle* and so many more. Motoring magazines are bit like motoring museums, diverse and eclectic in content.

Throw in the vintage tractor movement, the rise of commercial classic vehicle enthusiasm, and the sub-culture expands – as do the museums to feed it.

On-line magazines also provide easy access to the old car and old motorcycle narrative and involvement. And what is wrong with taking your digital device to a museum and looking at it as you tour? Well, surely this is as 'wrong' as using your mobile phone or tablet in the cinema or worse, at a restaurant! Please, if you do this and think it is normal, then (a) it is not, (b) stop it.

Up and down the country, clubs and owners gather at museums in order to share in the great automotive excitement. Modellers and pedal-car enthusiasts are not left out at many motor museums either. And neither should they be.

Visiting the big museums and delving into their archives is some of the best fun to be had, but so too is visiting some of the smaller, lesser known museums where we can commune with cars in a different way. You will find them herein. Something called 'adult learning' now also takes place at museums. What that means is that petrol heads old and young can go on a course or a seminar and learn how to restore old cars, or research their histories, or learn how to write about the subject. Oh, and there are 'restoration workshops' too – great oily-rag stuff!

The American Collier Collection in Florida provides the enthusiast and researcher with a great example of how to promote an archive. The Foundation's work saw the rise of the Revs Institute from 2010, an archive and library service with digital and on-line access. Nearly 20,000 books and nearly half a million photographs can be accessed at the Foundation. A link to Stanford University (California campus) provides the Collier Collection/Revs Institute with an academic tangent to motoring research – one that we are sure to see becoming increasingly important to the automotive historian, the enthusiast and the archivist. Revs 2 – the expansion of the Revs Institute is set to make a major mark on American marque history.

Major car manufacturers have created 'heritage' divisions and their own museums and research facilities. The National Motor Museum offers a dedicated motoring research service; the British Motor Industry Heritage Trust also offers superb archival services – where the Jaguar-Daimler Heritage Trust also offers a great mechanism for research.

Charitable trusts seem to be on the rise as do libraries available to members of car clubs and the likes of the Vintage Sports-Car Club and the Veteran Car Club have library facilities. The Society of Automotive Historians has a global reach via its British and main S.A.H. bases in the USA. Australia, South Africa, Asia, and South America, all operate thriving 'old car' museums and club movements and many rare and specific finds lie with them.

Cars, aircraft, locomotives, ships, steam engines, tractors, motorcycles, in fact anything with a mechanical function, an engineering action, an industrial design, seems to capture us, especially if it is old – from the age when driving was real, and interaction between man (or women) and mechanical machine was not a dreaded 'fly-by-wire' deviant of digital authoritarianism.

Who knows what the next decades will bring for the motor car, but we will always have that epoch of the twentieth century and its motoring as preserved by our museums: I urge you to support our car museums and get involved.

One way to help our museums beyond paying to get in, or holding your car club's meeting at a museum, is to volunteer, and also to use their archives for research. You would be amazed who you might meet amongst the volunteers. I was researching at Brooklands and found myself deep in conversation with an elderly volunteer who had turned up in a Mineral Blue MGB GT. His name was Christopher Orlebar and he was once a Concorde and VC10 pilot and British Airways captain. Sadly, he has recently passed on, but there are others like him out there amid the cars with gripping stories to tell. Concorde pilots can also be found loitering at the Bristol Aerospace and transport museum. We cannot discuss Brooklands, its brilliance without a man named Alan Winn who has recently retired from Brooklands, for Alan played a pivotal role in Brooklands development as a museum and more.

Bill Little's wonderful private collection was open once a year and packed out with bikers and admirers as well as petroliana and artefacts.

And you never know who you might bump into at an autojumble; can you think of anything that is as much fun as an autojumble, with a nice warm museum to go into for a cup of tea? Simple pleasures perhaps – but essential elements.

We still have many 'barn finds' to unearth. Every year, a new cache of forgotten cars is discovered, and restorers get to work; so too over-restorers who seem to want to obliterate a car's history and create a plasticised, vinyled, replication of a car and then call it 'original' and '100 points'. Surely, 'concours' is a term now often debased by the ruination of patina, and history of a car, its owners and their driving across the decades. You are free to disagree.

Cars are not villains

On an environmental note, we should all of course be cognisant of the realities of man-made pollution and its climate-change effects. But labelling old cars as 'polluters' is often unfair (unless two-stroke powered!). An average modern car creates approximately 30 tons of CO_2 during its manufacturing process per car. A large car or 4x4 may create over 100 tons of CO_2 during manufacture – per car. This is before even setting a wheel on the road. Old cars have *already* produced their manufacturing pollution and therefore buying one creates less CO_2-from-manufacture than a new car. Old car engines, providing that they are correctly maintained, are not generally excessive emitters of polluting airborne contaminants; they are not 'zero' emissions vehicles of course, but they are not always the 'devils' so often portrayed. Therefore, the preservation and use of old cars should not be seen as anti-environmental and especially not in light of recent new car emissions scandals. Old cars contain less plastic too!

Those people who *do* see old cars as such polluting devices do, of course, need to stop owning a car, travelling in or using any form of combustion engine-driven transport and, vitally, stop eating *any* food other than home-grown organic vegetable produce as the climate-change inducing and cancer-linked contaminants emitted by the industrial farming and food production process the world 'enjoys' are on a scale that rivals or exceeds that of the internal combustion engine. They also need to address the issue of pesticides, emissions, road-use and air travel within such food production and the flatulence inherent in the growing of the meat they eat. Animal rectal exhaust emissions are significant in meat production and a major environmental issue. It's just that they are less obvious than a bit of blue smoke from an old car's exhaust.

A single, short-haul (1,000 mile) flight in a typical jet airliner will emit 1.5 tons of CO_2 into the atmosphere. You would have to drive an economy car over 5,000 miles to even begin to approach that figure. Yet the emissions from the aircraft are invisible whereas those from the car are obvious and much complained about.

The Napier Railton in action at Brooklands. Not static, but firing. Brooklands Double Twelve action.

In Britain alone, the potential CO2 output from the fracking industry is reported to be going to equal the CO2 emissions from the lifetimes of 280 million cars. Yet fracking has been *encouraged* by government while car engines are attacked and taxed. The paradoxes and internal inconsistencies are many.

In the 1970s, huge, inefficient *grosser-wagen* 4x4s – now so common – were *not* used in an utterly unnecessary manner to tackle urban streets on the school run. Today they are – but driven by eco-campaigners, recycling fanatics, and rich 'new age' mums and dads who think they are 'green'. It is *so* bizarre.

I drive and restore old cars that emit pollutants, but I carbon-offset this by being vegetarian and eating non-chemical, locally-sourced organic and non-industrial food. So I invite critics of the old vehicle movement, to stuff their hypocrisy up their chemically induced exhaust pipes.

The fashion for electrifying old classic cars is another debate. Why would you pay £100,000 or more for an electrified, original Mini? Where is the point other than the assuaging of a conscience, and with the CO2 emitting power station generating the car's electricity, being *invisible* over the horizon?

Retrospective and cherry-picked judgement is hardly fair and it seems, is selectively being deployed by some anti-car campaigners. They attack the internal combustion engine that has actually liberated the world and many poor people from otherwise limiting lives, but conveniently ignore other pollution points. Most ships – tankers, cruise liners, and freight liners – pour out CO_2 and contaminants by the many tons, but they too are invisible in daily life, so the car gets it in the neck instead – again.

If we can achieve a *balanced* view and celebrate our vehicles, we can revel in the glory of their industrial design and their driving enjoyment.

We owe our museums much. So support our museums. Let's salute the volunteers who staff so many of our museums for, just like race marshals, without them, little would happen. The entries herein are listed alphabetically and by their main subject or purpose name – with 'The' marked as secondary, as for example, 'The Bugatti Trust' is listed under 'B' for Bugatti not 'T' for 'The'. The National Motor Museum Beaulieu is thus filed under 'N'.

I have avoided a museum contents list for every museum as this would be space limiting and subject to change, however, I have listed the most recent contents for major museums and selected delights of smaller museums.

A prior language applies to the design and engineering of our old cars. So, given the extensive use of in our museums of such now obscure descriptive terms for body styles in older vehicles, the reader may find the guide to coachbuilder/designers body style terminology, useful.

There is not much more to be said, other than to tell you that this book's recommendations are made upon the basis of experience and reviews, not on inducements.

Time to press the starter: pump some more petrol and get on with it.

Lance Cole
Wiltshire via Cornwall, Brittany, Africa, and Australia

1

MOTORING MUSEUM ESSENTIALS

The essential Riley excellence. Alan Ward's two-tone Riley on the move.

If we are going to spend time looking at vehicles from the past, it might be an idea to be fully conversant with the main eras, dates and the terminology used in such cars. So, without wanting to insult the intelligence of those in the know, or those of elevated status or 'cognoscenti' ego, here, provided for the enthusiast reader and for those willing to learn or refresh their thinking, is a quick reference guide (or reminder), to the eras and the key terminology applied to earlier cars as likely to be found in car museums.

We also need to know that the first British car museums were small, privately funded affairs – personal collections. Then came more organised gatherings and in 1952, the Edward Douglas-Scott-Montagu Motor Museum at Beaulieu was a precursor to a national movement and it too started with a private gathering of half a dozen cars. By 1959, nearly 300,000 members of the British public had visited the house and wooden sheds that constituted what was the nascent National Motor Museum at Beaulieu. From 1964, a dedicated new building and true major museum status acted as a kick-start to the wider 'national' museum context we know so well today.

The late John Haynes' passion for cars and motorsport remains a 'go to' on the 'must see' list. Newly revamped, the Haynes International Museum near Yeovil contains cars and themed displays that may need more than a day to get around. The dedicated motorsport displays at the Haynes Museum cannot but tug at the emotions of the motorsport fan. You cannot help but stand and stare and try to imagine the sight, sound and smell of the cars in action: are these cars, with their histories and patina, *really* inanimate objects incapable of telling their story?

We now have global, professional bodies or de facto 'authorities' that run our world of old, classic cars. The likes of the American Associations such as the Antique Automobile Club of America, assorted clubs, the *Federation Internationale des Vehicules Anciens* (FIVA), add much to our automobilia. The Federation of British Historic Vehicle Clubs (FBHVC) plays a huge role in promoting and supporting the use and driving of old cars from a British perspective in a business worth billions of pounds per year in the UK alone (£5.5billion at last count). A professional body supporting the smaller museums also exists –the Association of Independent Museums (AIM).

Motoring, or transport-related museums offer a specific niche and their authenticity is key to their survival. Also vital is our own understanding, and our willingness to learn. Museums are about learning, as well as seeing. 'I did not know that' is an often heard phrase in a car museum.

Interestingly, several marque clubs have set up their own museums; the Aston Martin Owners Club Heritage Trust Museum being a prime example. Bugatti fans have created the Bugatti Trust which is allied to the separate entity that is the very friendly Bugatti Owners Club. The French, Friends of Bedelia group must be encouraged to do the same thing for the Bedelia is not mad, it is marvellous.

Pre-war delight. Riley Sprite seen at Bicester Heritage on a great open day.

Meanwhile, the David Brown Tractor Club and their collection, prove that it is not all about cars.

Collections covering brochures, ephemera, engineering and design drawings, photographs and a myriad of documents charting the history of the car, all lie out there, awaiting our discovery. Interestingly, the digital age and twenty-first century technology provide the motoring investigator with huge gains – *Motor Sport* has placed its entire publication run as an archive in a vital digital web resource.

We have an amazing history to revel in. From Nicolas Cugnot who created the first 'car' or self-propelled vehicle in 1769 (if we ignore ancient Chinese claims to a inventing a propelled vehicle, and the designs of Leonardo da Vinci, to Karl Benz, to Ferdinand Porsche, from Henry Ford or Herbert Austin, from Ettore Bugatti to Gabriel Voisin, and the works of Sir Frederick Lanchester, the history of early motoring is infused with greatness. And was it not Camille Jenatzy who created in 1899 the early electric car – a streamlined 65mph device named '*La Jamais Contente*'? Did not Ferdinand Porsche invent axle-mounted hybrid electric motors at the turn of the nineteenth century in the Lohner-Porsche?

For the enthusiast, defined periods in this history of the automobile are set, but also subject to national colloquialism and terminologies. Familiarisation with their dated eras can only assist us on our museum visit. Knowledge of dates, eras, terms, design and engineering language, can be very helpful. The following are the terms and general 'nomenclature' that frame many exhibits in motoring museums and often seen.

Veteran

The Veteran period is from the start of motoring pre-1900 up to the year 1904. Also known in the USA as the 'Pioneer' era to certain observers. Although veteran and vintage are indeed universal terms, they mean different things in different countries, especially in the USA. In the USA a Veteran car is one produced between 1906-1912. An American 'Vintage' car definition refers to one manufactured between 1912 and 1929 whereas the British define Veteran cars as those built *before* 31 December 1904! And Vintage cars come after the Edwardian classification.

Edwardian

A lesser-used definition to describe a period post-1904 up to 1918 yet which ignores for the purpose of history and fashion, the date that the relevant King Edward VII came to the throne and the date of his death in 1910. Generally deemed to run up to the start of the First World War, when car design and manufacture effectively stalled for the duration.

Vintage

The defined period of car production from 1905 to 1930, yet which has been slightly extended into the 1930s by some. The British Vintage car period runs from 1919 to the last day of 1930. A Post-Vintage car can, say some, cover the era just beyond to 1939.

Thoroughbred or Post-Vintage Thoroughbred

Applied by some to the post-vintage era cars of 1931-1939. Once cited in the title of *Thoroughbred and Classic Cars* magazine – now *Classic Cars*.

Post-War and Classic

Defines a generic era 1945 through to the late-1960s of 'classic cars' but open to interpretation. In the Second World War, little car design focus took place and 1939-1945 currently lacks a defined classification beyond 'war-time production'. The same thinking applies to books as produced to 'war-time standard'. Included within the post-war era can be 'thoroughbred' cars whose origins lie in the very late-1930s. The defined niche 'Post-War' cars of 1946-1959 are also 'classics', yet the wider generic term 'classic car' encompasses the post-war era well into the 1960s.

Old-timer

A Northern European/German term for any very old veteran and early vintage era car.

Modern Classic

A more recent term to describe cars of the 1970s and up to the 1980s and perhaps beyond.

Young timer
Another northern European/Germany for a modern classic.

Of particular note, many museums and collections use descriptions of cars in terms of their engineering and design that require more than a passing knowledge of the history of car design. The reader may be assisted in their visits to see or research cars, by the inclusion herein of key terms that are used by car collectors, car collections and museums to categorise the myriad of earlier car types, styles, and design features.

Car body design/coachbuilder terminology:
Aero-screen
Small square or semi-circular/ellipsoid windscreen mounted on the scuttle of an open car type to reduce wind resistance but still proved some form of occupant shielding from the wind. Also as a racing car fitment.

Barrel-sided
A form of body design where there can be found a convex curve-under shape to bodysides towards the lower panels (sills) as a turn-under shape leading to a barrel-shaped curvature. Not to be confused with tumblehome.

Beetle-back
Not related to the VW 'Beetle' but an earlier term to describe a rounded tail or roof line that suggested the rear contours of an insect/beetle (carapace).

Berline/Berlina
Often applied to a French, German or Italian car, this means standard saloon – four-doors. A horse-drawn carriage term, 'Berlin' evolved into the modern era. A Berline is a French term, but Berlina is the Italian etymology but a Berlinetta is a smaller, (often two-seat) sports coupé version of a Berlina (such as a Ferrari Berlinetta). Germans still however refer to a mid-range saloon as 'Berlina'.

Boat-tail(ed)
Refers to a touring-type body that has a pointed tail end, aping the (converse) prow of a small boat or rowing boat, or a pointed boat stern (not all sterns are pointed and many are flat-backed).

Boat-decked
Indicates that wood or 'decking' has been applied to the upper surface of a top panel – overlaid as in boat building practice and notably for stern decks.

Brake (Shooting)/Break

The early term for an estate car body type and describing the rugged and large vehicles used for taking shooting guests to upper class shoots and to carry their guns, dogs and kit. Also as a car to collect cargo and baggage in the country from railway stations to return to one's estate hence the derivation of 'Station Wagon' still extant in the USA. Originally the 'Shooting Brake' this is the origin of today's estate car. Of note, the French term for such cars was, and remains, a 'Break' of alternative spelling. The Swedish and Germans often refer to such cars as 'Wagonettes' and this has transposed to the U.S. colloquialism of 'Wagon' to describe an estate car or hatchback – beyond the use of the earlier 'station wagon'.

Buggy

Applied to short-wheelbase two-seater chassis body combinations of simple and horse-cart derived style.

Cabriolet

A confusing and multiply used term to describe a partially folding roof with proper weather protection and one supported by an inner mechanism and or removable panels, but not a true lightweight roadster-type soft top of minimal accommodation as latterly framed.

The true word cabriolet has differing usage in Britain, the USA and Europe dependent on era. The inter-war British practice was to apply the term to a sports-specified large saloon often with four-doors – so British cabriolets of the 1920s and 1930s were larger, four-seat and, sometimes, four-door affairs with folding roofs of greater weather protection than a normal open car. As late as the 1950s, Rolls-Royce and various coachworks such as Hooper were still producing large, four-door soft-tops in the Anglicised cabriolet idiom; the 1952 Rolls-Royce Hooper-bodied Silver Wraith Cabriolet being a stunning and advanced example (the Gulbenkian car). Beyond 1965, the Lincoln Continental of the US Presidential fleet defined a specific cabriolet context so different from the central European coupé-cabriolet sports car type. The Lincoln was the last true grand saloon cabriolet of the pre-war style carried over.

Prior to 1940, giants such as the 1930s Bentley, Rolls-Royce, Horch, and Mercedes-Benz offerings were all 'cabriolets' despite their massive sizes and engine capacities, the controversial Mercedes 'Grosser' model of 7.7 litres being an example. But today, cabriolet means a different type of car in a new context.

'Three-quarter' cabriolets, and 'single' cabriolets were also defined according to type, accommodation and roof functions. A 'faux' cabriolet was just that, a falsely trimmed fixed roof device that hinted at being foldable but was not.

An American cabriolet category also exists and defines a soft-roofed front or driver's compartment and a fixed, hard-roofed rear saloon. A 'salamanca' cabriolet was a Spanish-designed Rolls-Royce type with luxury interior.

Later, smaller or specific cabriolets of differing types included the Porsche 356 and Jaguar XJ-S. And was the Fiat 125 soft-top a cabrioletot a convertible?

Cant rail
The portion of a car's roof at each side; running from the A pillar rearwards.

Carrosserie/Carrozzeria/Karrossen
The French, Italian and German terms respectively for a car body designer and specialist coachbuilder as a company or service beyond a manufacturer's output. It was common to send a car chassis from its maker to a specialist body-builder. In English, the term coachbuilder stemmed from horse drawn and railway stock design and fabrication and was transferred to specialist non-factory marque, car and vehicle body design and building.

Cape-cart
Derived from the South African style of small horse-drawn 'Cape' cart. Applied to the motor car circa 1905- 1910 as a description of a specific type of folding, fabric or leather hood with a collapsible timber support structure.

Cloverleaf
A description of staggered-type three seat cabin layout with two seats to the front and one centrally to the rear as in the planform of a three-leafed cloverleaf

Close-coupled
An old-fashioned term that defines a smaller cabin or shorter wheelbase in which the front and rear seats have lesser or minimal legroom.

Club/Club Brougham
An American term applied to formal, upright-styled, upmarket, fixed-head, solid roofed cars circa 1920. A 'Brougham' derived from British horse drawn cart days (after Lord Brougham) and then became used in the USA where it was deployed as a marketing tag to define a formal saloon type of upmarket or badge-engineered car. This carried on into the modern car era of the 1980s. A shorter-bodied Brougham of the vintage era can be termed a 'Single Brougham'.

Coupé
Deriving from the French term (hence the é accent used outside of the USA) coupé meaning to 'cut' and thus describing a smaller, or shortened body form as latterly

applied to sports cars or two-door coupés. Earlier applied to larger or four-seat, four-door cars with a specific, drop-head or fixed-head roof style. Some 1920s coupés were in fact large car types and *not* in the form of the modern understanding of the term.

The three-quarter coupé was a closed, two-door, two-seater with an upright cabin and a third seat mounted externally at the rear as in a 'dickey' seat.

Doctor's coupé was an early term that lasted into the 1930s and which described a car of more sporting style and often a two-seater. High-built with large doors and plenty of luggage space, they became popular with the medical profession and hence doctor's coupé. Other coupé iterations also existed – including a 'golfer's' coupé and a 'victoria' coupé. An 'opera' coupé was an American, four-seater with only two doors and small rear windows – latterly 'opera' windows. A 'fixed-head' coupé was a 1920s-1930s fashion now obscured by the more generic, smaller, fastback idiom of the coupé.

A 'drop-head' coupé is now a 'convertible' but in cars past, it was a coupé type but with a folding roof. Many vintage-era and pre-war classic cars of four-seater open-top design are still definitively referred to as 'drop-head' coupés, and yet so too are 1950s and 1960s two seater sports cars!

Coupé de Ville is a term related to use in the Sedanca type nomenclature, this term described a sportier, or grander luxury sports derivative of a body-on-chassis design, also applied as a fixed-head to very large cars and exemplified by the grandiose 1927 T41chasis Bugatti Coupé Napoleon. The 'de Ville' is a nominative term deriving from its use in 'town' (ville) car description (see below).

Cowl

The America term for the scuttle or firewall/bulkhead in the front cabin structure of the car. In the UK, a cowl is an especially shaped covering or form over an area or mechanical feature, notably on an engine. 'Cowl-flap' is a movable panel to aid cooling in an engine compartment of an aircraft or vehicle.

Cyclecar

A lightweight car derived from early cycle car chassis and engine type as a light car: the basis of many interesting smaller types as *voiturette*-cycle cars and a derivation into a lightweight two-seater sporting type of circa 1920.

De Capotable/Decouvrable

The purist French term for a convertible, soft-roofed car type, literally 'uncoverable' or revealable in context. Last really framed by the Citroën DS De Capotable by Henri Chapron.

de Ville

From the French 'de ville' (of the town) and applied to a certain, upright limousine body type often used in town or city guise in early motoring when unpaved roads

rarely extended beyond suburbia's limits. A de ville featured an opening roof of the front cabin or driver and front passenger or chauffeur's compartment. This could be folded, slid, or removed when out of the town and free of traffic or the public's gaze. A formal car design type and description applied mainly prior to 1925. In the USA, a sedanca de ville was a town car of slightly more sporting luxury design and marketing.

Dog-cart
An early open car with a high rear deck of taller proportions, again taking its style from horse-drawn cart design practice. Large driven wheels often featured as did a rear panel access door. An early form of 'ute'.

Dos-a-dos
A French-originated term for a car with two rows of seats configured in back-to-back formation of *dos a dos* or back to back.

Duck(s)back
An especially formed and shaped rear body design with pointed tail and undercut lower form. Not unlike the rear underside of a duck – hence the terminology. Synonymous with the 1920s Alvis 12/series Tourer types.

Fishtail
An American term to describe a sharper body line of the boat-tail iteration.

Forecar
A very early veteran-type car in which the front seats were mounted ahead of the wheelbase and front axle in an early 'forward control' type configuration. Some such types had the driver mounted behind the front passenger seats.

High-Wheeler
An American term applied to a taller, larger, buggy-type fitted with larger diameter or high wheels for country use.

Kamm-back
Applied to the 'cut-off' or 'sliced' rear bodywork of otherwise long-tailed or tear-drop shaped car bodies. Created as an device of aerodynamic drag reduction and wake vortex control by Professor Wunibald Kamm, the Swiss-German road-vehicle aerodynamicist active in Stuttgart in the 1930s, alongside his colleague R. von Koening Fachsenfeld, and still applied to hatchbacks, sports cars and racing cars.

Landau/Landaulette

Description of a formal, grand car of many seats often used for VIP and State usage and deriving or adopted from horse-drawn Landau grand carriage types. Many seen with opening roof sections and VIP rear compartments. Often fitted with a division or partition between the owners or VIP rear-compartment and the 'staff' chauffeur at the driving seat. Extra rear glazing and a folding rear roof allowed the elevated-status passengers to be seen by the populace. Many derivatives of the Landau exist and a smaller-sized such car is a Landaulette, both types being prolific in the Edwardian era. Last seen in service in the British royal household.

Limousine

Associated in current British minds as VIP or State vehicle, the term originally applied to many formal, saloon types of cars on both sides of the Atlantic. Limousine derives from a term stemming from the French practice of the Limousin area to create a protective or all-weather encapsulation for the hoods of horse-drawn carriages – soon easily transferred to the early grand saloon car.

A Limousine de Ville describes a large VIP or upmarket-type vehicle – specifically one which in the vintage era, would have had an open-roofed front cabin section. The Sedanca de Ville took over as the colloquial term for such cars from the Limousine de Ville post-1939.

In Germany however, a limousine defines a large, executive saloon car and remains a term of such context.

Monocoque

The term for a self-supporting car body of integral, all-welded one-piece construction in which the body parts each link to each other to form a one-piece body shell that does not require a separate chassis or subframe. Can also apply to a one-piece moulded composite-type shell. Note however that part-monocoque steel bodies can be mounted to some form of underframe, notably in the American market practice.

Monoposto

A single-seat car, post-1925 after riding mechanics were deleted, and often cited as a racing or hard core sports car in the early 'Grand Prix' iteration.

Opera (window)

Originally a rear-compartment opening quarter light window each side of the car at the front of the main rear passenger compartment. Latterly a 1950s-1980s styling term for the small window seen in the C or D-pillars of American and Japanese cars as a styling affection. Used in 1960s US car ranges as a circular window – port-hole

fashion – and used more rationally in the Saab 99/900 five-door body shell as a small, curved rear window in the D-pillars to improve visibility.

Phaeton

Originally, a phaeton was a sporty horse-drawn carriage but the name was carried over to early (veteran) car 'open' body design, often seen in conjunction with a folding tonneau cover. Subsequently, a phaeton became a larger, grander body type of elegance and grand proportions aping a limousine in some senses. Some open phaetons had a second windscreen mounted at the front of the main rear seating compartment. Single phaeton, double phaeton and triple phaeton were all distinct variations, describing how many seat rows the cabin contained. A sport phaeton was a shorter, more stylish shape often seen with a boat-type tail.

Pullman

A luxe or luxury definition of a grand comfort saloon car – derived from railway coaches of luxury type.

Quarter Light

Originally defined as a small openable or movable window at the rear cabin of a large vintage-era pre-1939 car. Post-1945, a quarter light became known as a front-quarter light – an openable, swivel-mounted small triangular window mounted at the leading edge of the front side windows directly adjacent to the windscreen or A-pillar to increase ventilation flow into the cabin. Now rarely seen on modern cars.

Razor-edge(d)

A body design where the exterior edges and panels were of sharp-edged and square cut design and setting that could also be blended with curves. Used from the 1930s up to the 1950s in American and British contexts. A notable Rolls-Royce feature via coachbuilders Freestone & Webb, Hooper, Park Ward, Mulliner, Thrupp & Maberly and James Young. Also seen in 'windswept' and reverse-angled body styles. Some razor-edge designed were long, sporty and elegant, but shorter bodies of razor-edge tended to be upright, formal and somewhat truncated. The Triumph Mayflower was a strange and late attempt at razor-edge styling mixed with other ideas.

Roadster

An MGB soft-top can be called a roadster, but so too can a Bugatti T55 Sport – for a roadster is a sporty open car with two seats. Within that definition, many variations of the roadster description could apply.

Roi de (Belges)

An upmarket type of coachbuilt body named after Kong Leopold II of the Belgians. Featured luxury seating in a tall-side open body of grand, State impression. Also used under-curved body shaping and side panels and flaring to produce a 'Tulip' shaped body design effect that was also applied to other car types (notably in an early F. Porsche design)

S-irons

The curved hinges of S-shape as external brackets that were mounted upon the sides of a folding roof/hood and which held this in tension when erected. Subsequently used as a gargoylesque non-functioning trim item up until the 1970s in American and Japanese cars.

Sedanca

A large, luxury-trimmed saloon type description given to much erroneous attribution and application. Often very expensive and in the 1920s-30s, a favourite style of the British coachbuilding scene as sold to the rich and the landed gentry and royalty.

A Sedanca de ville was such a saloon car that had been modified with a removable front roof section (only). Numerous other sedanca terminology exists. A true Sedanca is a coupé of sweeping lines and sporting elegance. Stems from a Spanish origin of a one-off design type; now a forgotten term yet one that lasted from 1920 through to the 1960s.

Scuttle & Scuttle-shake (USA: Cowl)

The mid-portion of the car around and beneath the windscreen and firewall bulkhead. Scuttle-shake applies to soft-top cars, mostly where the pre-existing roof has been removed to create a convertible type and insufficient bracing has been applied leading to body flex at the scuttle.

Skiff

The delightful description applied to swept or sculpted bodywork in the manner of a water-borne hydrodynamic boat shape. Often used in tourer and torpedo bodywork. Metal or timber-clad, the skiff body can be large or small, but is often elegant and possessed of prow or stern shaping.

Spider

An early term used circa 1905 for a small, lightweight two-seat open car that drew its inspiration from sporty, two-seat horse-drawn carriages of such iterations, but then revived in the 1920s and again in the 1960s to describe a lightweight open-two seater with basic weather equipment such as hand-operated folding roof (e.g.: Fiat 124, and various Italian and French types). Always a 'Spider' in the Italian and French market.

Spyder
A different (Northern European) spelling of the above type and description, often erroneously applied. Not to be confused with Spyker or Spijker.

Streamliner
The evocative term that rose in the 1920s to the 1930s to describe cars with faired, in-curved, aerodynamically inspired bodies often with ellipsoid tear-drop forms and tail sections. Often curvaceous and with merged contours, but still seen with separate drag-inducing mudguards or wings. Evolved into a series of two-door coupé types, and four-door saloon types with streamlined or air flow bodies. At its height, a French flamboyant styling movement, at its more prosaic, the production of 'fastbacked' and 'air-line' swept body styles on standard saloons such as Rover, MG, and others of the 1930s. Also applied to racing cars, exotics, and special 'streamliners' and perhaps defined pre-1939 by output from Mercedes-Benz, Alfa Romeo, VW, and Porsche.

Surrey
A body type taken from horse drawn carriage types and fitted with a decorative canopy roof – also colloquially cited as a 'Surrey-on-top'. Better known in the USA.

Tandem
Not just a bicycle with front and rear seating, but also a light car with in-line seating, often with the driver at the rear (as in the wonderful Bedelia).

Targa
A description of a roof design where the A, or B, or C pillars remain in-situ 'fixed-head' but an open-air effect is created by removing a very central large roof panel or divided roof panels (only) leaving the rear and rear side screens in place. Often associated with modern classics of the 1960s-1970s era (Porsche 911, Triumph TR4, and Stag, Datsun 260Z), an early application was by the Saab designer Sixten Sason in a 1950s prototype. The idea stems from the Edwardian era of removable roof panels in fixed-head bodies. Peugeot designer Jean Andreau experimented with such ideas, and electric folding metal roof panels, as early as the 1930s.

Toast-rack
A four-door touring type body with no doors but access cut-outs – giving rise to the appearance of a rack – hence, toast rack.

Tonneau
Derived from the French term *tonneau* describing a cask or barrel. This shape was applied in early veteran era coachbuilding to the rear of car bodies, hence 'half-tonneau'. A rear-entrance door was a common feature. A 'double-tonneau'

indicated a larger, four-seat rear cabin. Note: not to be confused with tonneau-cover which is a leather or synthetic weather-covering often with attachment studs, that is supplied with 'open' cabin cars and soft-top sports cars.

Top Hat
A styling trick where an upright roof has a vertical rear panel yet it is curved in side profile and top-plate profile to blend the roof and cabin together. The rear panel is curved across the rear of the car yet blends into a convex roof dome. Seen in the 1934 Rolls-Royce Phantom Continental by Freestone & Webb coachbuilders, but also regurgitated in a recent Renault Megane design – with curved rear valance and vertical rear window and roof combinations.

Torpedo
A body design that featured side panels and body line of constant height, often with some form of shaping to the front and rear sections of the vehicle. The sides were high and the seat back hidden from line of sight. Not really meant to be associated with streamline or curved bodies as in the shape of a hydrodynamic torpedo despite the name and inherent potential of such. However if streamlined wings or nose shaping were added, a sports-torpedo was more obvious.

Tourer
A widely interpreted generic term for an 'open' car with multiple door access. Often associated with folding-roof cars. Now more widely or loosely applied to a certain type of car in the context of its design, intended use, market sector and power rating. A sports-tourer was a sharper, close-coupled body design, but early pre-1925 tourers were more formal and offered greater comfort and weather protection. The 'Touring' or touring car (USA) body became a defined fashion prior to 1939.

Note; not to be confused with the name and output of the Italian bodywork/coachbuilding concern 'Carrozzeria Touring' as a company.

Tricar
An early three-wheel car or three-wheeler circa 1880-1910 designed on horse drawn cart lines but equipped as a 'horseless carriage' with the new-fangled internal combustion engine or steam engine. A specific 'tricar' type evolved using metal frames and tubes to create a device resembling a cross between a wheelchair, a bicycle and an early motorcycle.

Turret Top
An American late 1920s styling theme in which 1930s Buick's excelled. Featured an upright yet domed roof, smoothed onto a streamlined styled bod.

Tumblehome
An ancient medieval shipbuilders term that referred to the curvaceous or hip-like (feminine) rear view shape of a boat or ship hull that curved inwards towards the top of each side. This reduced surface area, lowered the centre of gravity and had hydrodynamic benefits. Latterly applied to veteran, vintage (and modern) car bodies to achieve similar effects in aerodynamic and design terms.

Ute
Mid-twentieth century Australian term for a pick-up (UK) type, or utility, small truck or car-based 'ute'. In Southern Africa, the type is known as a 'Bakkie'.

Victoria
Related to a horse drawn carriage term, applies to a two-seat early car often with a folding hood of 'Victoria Hood' description. An incongruous 'Sporting Victoria' hood was applied to very large early cars (Hispano-Suiza, Isotta Fraschnin etcetera), with a large, upright rear panel acting like a sail into the on-coming wind.

Vis-a-vis
Defines a four-wheeled car in which passengers were seated to face each other *vis a vis* (face-to-face in French) in opposing plan. Sometimes the driver was centrally mounted facing forward yet sat at the rear!

Voiturette
Voiturette derives from the French for car and was applied to light and cycle-car derived devices in early motoring and racing circles into the 1920s. An 'ette 'describes a lighter or smaller diminutive version of the voiture car hence voiturette.

Weymann (-bodied)
Coachbuilder who built ash-frame reinforced, fabric-bodied car bodies (often saloons). Paris-based under M. Weymann, but also British based in Surrey as a major supplier of 1920s-30s fabric-covered wooden bodies to the car industry. The 'Weymann' body' in its reduced fatigue-technique thus became an established term.

Armed with the preceding information, the reader is well equipped to understand the types and descriptions encountered during a motoring museum visit.

Further understanding may be assisted by a brief explanation of the coachbuilder's role in car manufacture. Today, only the super-rich can commission a special body to be built upon a pre-existing car chassis or underframe. In the vintage and classic car era, right up to the 1970s, it was still accepted and practice

Blue AC at Bicester on another fantastic Bicester Heritage day.

for some customers to commission an external, non-factory company to design and build a one-off' or limited-series production run of specially-designed bodies for their cars. Prior to 1939, it was quite normal to purchase a running chassis and to send it away to be clothed in a new body. This process gave rise to the great British and European coachbuilders or design houses – carrosserie, carrozzeria, and karrosserie – now so famed and revered in the world of the old car. Italian designer stylists – 'carrozzeria' and 'stablimenti' – came to the fore post-1945 and British and French coachbuilding and styling houses declined. Bertone, Farina – Pininfarina after 1958 – Ghia, Vignale, Touring, and Zagato, were the leaders, Guigario's Ital Design emerging latterly.

In Germany, Porsche, Reutter, Karmann etc, had factory works or design bureaus known as 'Bau'.

Some car manufacturers ranging from Allard, Alfa Romeo, Alvis, Riley, Rover, to Bugatti, Porsche, Peugeot, Citroën, VW, Fiat, Rolls-Royce, Hispano-Suiza, and

many more, sent their chassis direct from their factories to specialist body design and fabrication companies. Americans did the same thing but used the term of 'Custom' for their specialist car body building. Special up-market bodies as applied to Packard, Pierce Arrow, Dusenberg, Cadillac, Lincoln and Oldsmobile, aped the European process.

The key coachbuilders' names and their locations, that the reader will likely encounter in British museums, are thus briefly presented for quick reference:

Antem: Courbevoie, France. 1919-1955
Arnold: Manchester, UK. 1910-1948
Barker: London, UK. 1710-1954
Bertone: Turin, Italy 1930s to 2000s
Binder: Paris, France. 1904-1939
Brewster: Connecticut, USA 1810-1937
Carbodies: Coventry, UK. 1926-1954
Carlton: London, UK. 1926-1939
Castagna: Milan, Italy. 1920-1947
Chapron: Paris, France. 1928-1980
Charlesworth: Coventry, UK. 1929-1945
Corsica: London, UK. 1930s
Derham: Pennsylvania, USA 1880s-1950s
D'Ieteren: Brussels, Belgium. 1920s-1950s
Erdmann & Rossi: Germany. 1925-1930s
Farina (Pininfarina): 1926/1958- to date
Fernandes & Darrin: Paris, France. 1920s-1939
Figoni et Falaschi: Paris, France. 1930s
Flewitt: Birmingham: UK. 1905-1957
Freestone & Webb: London, UK. 1923- 1957
Galle /Baxter Galle: Paris, France. 1920s-1930s
Ghia: Turin, Italy: 1916-1970: to date (Ford)
Gill: London, UK. 1914- 1935
Gurney Nutting: London, UK. 1919-1945
Hooper: London, UK. 1805-1959
Jarvis: Wimbledon, UK.1920s-1930s
Karmann: Germany.1901- 2009 (VW)
Kellner: Paris, France.1920-1939
Labourdette: Paris, France. 1890s-1930s
Lancefield: London UK.1921-1948
LeBaron: Connecticut, USA. 1920-1948
Letourner & Marchand: Paris, France. 1912-1939
Mann Egerton: Norwich, UK. 1898-1939

Mayfair: London. 1920/1929-1958
Million Guyet: Paris, France. 1920s-1946
Mulliner, A.: Northampton, UK. 1890s-1939
Mulliner, H.J.: London, UK. 1900-1990s
Offord: London, UK 1791-1939
Papler: Germany: 1924-1933
Park Ward: London, UK. 1919-1961- to H.J. Mulliner
Ranalah: Merton, Surrey, UK. 1920s-1939
Reutter: Stuttgart, Germany.1920s-1960s
Rippon: Huddersfield, UK. 1905-1958
Salmons: Newport Pagnell, UK. 1820-1957
Saoutchik: Paris, France. 1905-1954
Sodomka: Czech Republic. 1895-1958
Southern Coachcraft: London, UK. 1930s
Thrupp & Maberly: London. 1760-1960s
Touring, Milan, Italy. 1925-1966
Van den Plas: Belgium. 1868-1930s.
Vanden Plas: London, UK. 1912-2000s
Van Voorne: Paris, France. 1920s-1939
Vesters & Neirinck: Brussels, Belgium. 1930s
Vignale. Turin, Italy. 1948-1973
Vincent: Reading, Berkshire, UK. 1805-1959
Walter. Folkestone, Kent. UK. 1920s-1939
Weymann: Paris, and Surrey UK. 1920s-1930s
Willoughby: Utica, New York, USA. 1919-1938
Windovers: London, UK.1796-1956
Young, J. Bromley, Kent, UK. 1908-1967
Zagato. Milan, Italy. 1919 to date
Zietz: Geneva, Switzerland. 1920s

Who knew?

Museums can tell us much, and as example, let's cite Birmingham's Sir Frederick William Lanchester – genius, aero-auto-mechanical pioneer who say some created (as the Lanchester brothers) the first truly British car in 1895. Frederick certainly developed an elliptical wing in 1894 (long before Ludwig Prandtl, and then Ernst Heinkel did the same and grabbed the historical headlines) and then in 1899 founded a car marque.

Lanchester car No.2 of 1897, was a two-cylinder, air-cooled engined device which drove the rear wheels through a longitudinal shaft and worm gearing. This was the first truly quiet car, and probably the first to have a magneto ignition. Lanchester used wick carburettors, air-cooled engines, designed a crankshaft

Down Memory lane at the Atwell-Wilson Museum. Austins and patina perfection.

Vintage excellence. Alvis boat-tailer or 'ducks back' rests in timeless repose at Bicester.

damper, a 'worm' final drive gear, and then created larger, water-cooled engine cars, one of which was owned by Rudyard Kipling.

Lanchester had ties to Daimler and BSA. Lanchester's highlights included his Petrol Electric Motorcar of 1926. Lanchester cars ceased production in 1931 and became a badge-engineered Daimler sub-brand until final demise in 1956.

Lanchester's story proves that our motoring history is special. Visit the Lanchester Museum and Library, at Coventry University to prove the point.

On my ramble around the museums of motoring, I learned much. Citing a few out-takes beginning with 'B' illustrates just what a museum can teach you.

I discovered Brooke – the East Anglian car. If you think that the Lotus is the only car ever manufactured in East Anglia, think again. From 1900 to 1913, the J.W. Brooke Company of Lowestoft, who were marine engineers, created their own type of cars, Brooke built three-cylinder 'flat or horizontally opposed engines with chain drive transmissions. They tested their six-cylinder car engine in one of their motor boats. Of note, Brooke created the world's first dished steering wheel design. A six-cylinder engine was built in 1903 and then a move to vertical, in-line engine configuration was used in a four-cylinder Brooke engined car. The famous 'swan' car of 1913 was built for a titled Indian aristocrat of Calcutta (Kolkata) and this featured a six-foot high swan sculpture on its bonnet with illuminated eyes and an exhaust vent that whistled through the swan's beak!

What on earth is a Bedelia – A French four-wheeled cyclecar (1909-25) of an apparent coffin or bath tub with the driver sat at the rear behind the passenger in tandem, chain driven, and sometimes with the passenger at the rear doing the

steering! A sort of light aircraft crossed with a fast motorcycle. Latterly with 'normal' seating and a three-speed gearbox and two-cylinder engine. Consult the *Club Les Amis de Bedelia* for more information on these wonderful devices. Eighteen Bedelias remain of the 3,000 designed and built by Robert Bourbeau and Henri Devaux from late 1908. It would be easy to become obsessed with these things. Bedelias are brilliant.

B is for Berliet – a truck maker, but from 1895-1939 a maker of cars. Berliets were built under licence in America by the American Locomotive Company as the 'Alco' branded marque. Berliet were absorbed in Citroën in 1967.

What is a bolide? Is it a shapely, possibly fast, wheeled or winged device or mechanical 'thing'? Is it a meteor of high speed seen in astronomy that has its

Saab 92-001 UrSaab 1947 prototype seen at the Saab Museum, Trollhattan. Note the Bugatti-inspired seats. The Saab Museum was a precursor to the new age of the museum and is highly recommended.

etymology in the Greek term for a missile or arrow which has lent its name and speed to a mechanical description? Or is it a French make of car (1899-1908) which at one stage in the early 1900s boasting a 12 cylinder horizontally-opposed engine, also manufactured in Belgium as Schoneck? But Bolide was also a short-lived American car derivation dating from 1969 in the form a prototype V8 Can-Am-based sports racer.

Blodgett – the wonderfully named Blodgett was an American car of 1922 created by the Blodgett Engineering and Tool Press Company of Detroit, Michigan. Only one prototype was built with disc-wheels and a six-cylinder in-line Continental engine

Who has ever heard of the Danish car? Enter the 1904 Bukh and Gry and its water-cooled, 10hp two-cylinder engine, a car exhibited at the Tivoli in Copenhagen in 1905. Its engineers built their car after returning from working in car factories in the USA.

Bushbury Electric? This was a British company of 1897 who built electric three- and four-wheeled cars at the Star Cycle Company factory in Wolverhampton. Of note, some of these cars were steered by pulling on leather reins – as opposed to the then fashionable tiller

Our out-take into the entry of automotive history illustrates just what gems lie out there in the world of automania and its museums and archives. To discover this kind of information, you have to look, and only museums and books can provide such knowledge transfer.

Motorcycle Moments

The term 'bike' is now widely acceptable, but herein the preferred terminology of 'motorcycle' will be adhered to. Old motorcycles are categorised in a manner similar to old cars. Veteran, antique, and classic are the three category definitions, but they are a movable feast it seems. And 'Café Racer' is also a flexitarian option.

Motorcycle museums now abound. Britain, Italy, and Germany boast many, Japan is catching up. The motorcycle niche is addictive and often served in 'car' museums. Strangely, some car enthusiasts do not get excited by two-wheeled wonders, but the old motorcycle movement is growing, and they are of course, cheaper to purchase than the many of today's main stream classic cars as that pricing and value bubble brews.

A veteran motorcycle is one manufactured prior to 1915, and a vintage motorcycle is one manufactured after January 1915. However, in America and parts of Europe, some blurring of the line of dating and terminology can occur. Confusingly, a definition of a 'vintage' motorcycle that comes from the American Historic Racing Motorcycle Association cites pre-1970s motorcycles as vintage! Yet according to the Antique Motorcycle Club of America, an 'antique' motorcycle

is one that is 35 years old or more! State laws and accepted descriptions also vary between states. In some, a 25 year old motorcycle is 'antique'! Such blurring of the lines tends to sow the seeds of international confusion: just what will happen to the 'café racer' age-related definition is anyone's guess.

To add further to the global confusion, what constitutes 'vintage' varies across the motorcycle marques and between enthusiasts and owners. The Vintage Japanese Motorcycle Club now defines 'vintage' as a motorcycle being 15 years or older. However, for many western enthusiasts, only motorcycles made before the Second World War are true vintage bikes.

Café racer? Back in the 1950s, riders known as 'Rockers' would modify their bikes for speed, with lower handlebars, and more changes, riding quickly from nightspot to nightspot – usually a café, and without an accent on the e! This is where our framework of the cafe racer comes from. 'Mods' meanwhile would ride mopeds and sometimes even scooters. A cafe racer in Britain means a modified old motorcycle, yet there is also a more modern iteration of the modified machine as a modern cafe racer definition.

A classic motorcycle, rather in the vein of a classic car, tends to be dated from 1939 to the 1970s, although post-1970s modern classics are not yet as clearly defined within the movement.

A growing consensus among motorcycle enthusiasts is that any motorcycle over 25 years old could be considered as a 'classic', but some enthusiasts also frame their definition upon a more modern motorcycle's design features.

The century-plus of the British motorcycle is categorised into distinct eras and dates:

Pioneers 1899-1920
Vintage 1920-1940
Classic Era 1940-1970
Modern Classics 1970-1980s

A more specific 'modern classics' sub-culture also exists and covers:

Japanese Classics:
An emerging movement of the universal Japanese motorcycle.

American Classics:
A growing movement with flexible dates allowed.

East European/Soviet Classics:
A niche movement.

Citroen 5hp at the Lakeland Museum, Cumbria. (Photo: Lakeland Museum)

Some highlights of motorcycle design history

There is much we can learn at a museum, and the following out takes illustrate vignettes of the stories that are framed in the museum-led journey of discovery.

The Daimler Einspur ('single track')/Reitwagen ('riding wagon') of 1885 is cited as the original true motorcycle, after various powered bicycle designs including steam-powered iterations. The Daimler-Maybach designed machine had essential ingredients such as chain-drive, a frame, and a single-cylinder petrol engine – and yet it was a precursor to *car* design.

Alternatively, Edward Butler's design for a true motorised-cycle as a tri-cycle precursor motorcycle must be considered as the starting point of British motorcycle emergence at the same time. The first commercially successful recognisable motorcycle was the 1894 machine of Hildebrand and Wolfmuller in Germany. The British market had been suffering from 'Red Flag' and 'Locomotive' Acts that limited speed on the new public highways – which stifled vehicle and motorcycle design, thankfully soon lifted in 1896.

Curiously, the British early motorcycle builders used the more advanced French engines built under licence for the early British motorcycles *circa* 1900. Yet as early as 1899, the Holden motorcycle deployed a water-cooled four-cylinder motorised cycle.

We should also note the subcategories of 'American cruisers', 'Britbikes' and 'Classic bikes'.

A few key names:

BMW – 1922. Prior to becoming a car manufacturer in 1928, BMW made aircraft engines and early motorcycles, notably an almost-500c 'boxer' horizontally opposed engine with shaft drive as the first bug 'R' series motorcycle.

Ducati – Italy's essential motorcycle icon.

Harley-Davidson – 1906. This is where the art of the American motorcycle began, way back before the First World War. Early Harleys were single-cylinder, but as early as 1909, a. 810cc V-twin was manufactured.

Honda – 1950s. The true origins of the Japanese motorcycle industry saw Honda produce the 49cc Honda 50 Super Cub/C100 and create the profits and knowledge to go further into the 1970s 1,000cc horizontally-opposed 'Gold Wing' branding, and onwards to more recent stunning offerings.

Kawasaki, Yamaha – 1960s-1970s-1980s. The true era of the classic Japanese motorcycle ranging from high-powered 600-900cc bikes such as the Kawasaki H2, to the likes of the Yamaha DT1 as the first true Japanese 'dirtbike'.

Matchless – 1902. The true British innovator run by the Collier family based in London not Birmingham or Coventry. First use of front-tube-mounted engine. Produced a JAP-engined V-twin in 1905 and by 1912 had defined this as the true British design hallmark that many followed.

Meggla – 1922. Long before Dr Felix Wankel's works in cars, Meggla produced a rotary-cycle engined, front-wheel-drive, aerodynamically styled, advanced true motorcycle, yet as many have stated, rather like the flying wing or all-wing configuration of early aviation, it became a design diversion against mainstream narratives.

Moto Guzzi – 1950s. The dawn of Italian motorcycle design as exquisite longitudinal V-twin engineering. The less esoteric Falcone mobilised post-war Italy. Also the era of Ducati and 1960s racing exploits.

Norton – 1902. Another defining British motorcycle first manufacturing a James L. Norton designed motorcycle in 1902 – belt driven 3½hp, yet capable of 80mph. Norton began producing his own-design engines with rugged, simple design and good cooling in 1908, and the rest became history. Of note, Norton designed and built a very successful Wankel rotary-engined motorcycle (the Commander) which won the British Formula One and Shell Supercup, and led the TT. It redefined frame design via the 'featherbed' frame type.

NSU – 1900s-1950s. Defining period of Neckarsulmner Stricken Union motorcycle output that included aerodynamically faired racers of R. von Koneing-Fachsenfeld design, and Wankel type rotary valves and engine experimentation. Also lower cost machines for the masses.

Triumph – 1930s. Triumph (a bit like the modern British royal family) was founded rather ironically by two British-resident Germans. This happened in 1885 and Triumph produced its first true motorcycle in 1905 after motorised bicycle attempts in 1902-03. Within two decades, the defining Speed Twin set the pre-1939 mark for Triumph motorcycles and via its Turner design, led to the post-war epoch of Triumph motorcycles with machines such as the 650cc Bonneville. Triumph cars, under Standard-Triumph, BMC and BL, became another story.

The period also saw the development of the British motorcycle and its military applications. Also the era of the Brough and the key output of Birmingham and the Midlands motorcycle industry.

Vespa, Velo et al – 1940s. Here lies the dawn of the moped or scooter of French and Italian genius.

Vincent (Black Shadow) – 1949. Arguably the defining of British motorcycle 'bikedom' and the fastest road machine of its era. Of note, it used aircraft-style stressed member frame components thus eliminating a heavy frame as a *de facto* chassis. Philip Vincent followed this up with the Black Prince – with its regretably then unfashionable full 'aero' fairing. But Black Prince like the Black Shadow was exquisite in its engineering – as were Black Knight and the Rapide and wider Vincent range. Vincent closed in 1955 – but not before Mr Vincent had invented an built a water-scooter that predated today's jet-skis by years.

Aerial, Brough, BSA, James, Lea Francis,Norton, Triumph, Douglas, Rudge, Velocette, etcetera – The British 'greats' cover the epoch from single-cylinder to 'Gold Star', 'Superior' eras and beyond into the 1970s, and in some cases reincarnation today. From Aerial's first true motorcycle of 1902 to the famous names of the 1930s, 1950s and 1960s, the great decades of British motorcycle manufacturer are well known. But we should not forget smaller, early players like Cotton of Gloucester, BAT (Bat) of Penge, and the Wilkinson – built by the Wilkinson razor blade company! And of course there were smaller marques of the Midlands like Chater Lea, Clyno, Excelsior, Singer, Zenith, etcetera, which created the essential crucible of Bitish motorcycle genius until its infamous decline.

Zundapp made excellent German motorcycles, yet Horex, another German firm, also turned out Zundapp-badged Horex machines for export in the USA.

What of V-twins or Vee-twins? Italian manufacturer Ducati makes a V-twin, but the cylinders are narrower angled at 90 degrees (an L-twin they say) not 60 degrees as is also found in some engines. V-twins are also known for their unique burbling sound. And the best of British Vee-twins? There are many stories to be told.

Motorcycle categories:
Airhead
A BMW-specific term applied to BMW's air-cooled, flat-twin engines popular between 1923-95.

Bagger
Any machine equipped with saddlebags hanging from it.

Bobber
A customised bike, stripped down.

Cafe Racer
A dated term for dated motorcycles say some – but also the wider definition of a modified non-exotic older or, newer motorcycle tweaked for sports use and design delight.

Chopper
Defined by design and stance if not engine type. 1970s origins. Extended front suspension and cruising tweaks are assumed ingredients.

Cruiser
Low slung, long wheelbase, forward bias rider position, pull-back handlebars, softer riding and torque-ridden in all senses. Often of V-twin configuration. Real 'burblers'.

Custom
One-off or limited series of personally or manufactured modified motorcycles. Often of art-type design and paintwork as well as mechanical modifications. A major American movement.

Military
Modified or specially-designed motorcycles for military use, first conceived 1914-18, with sidecars coming to the fore. Specific output 1939-45.

Naked
Sport-type motorcycles essentially pared-down and devoid of any bodywork. Can also be applied to modified other types.

Sloper
A term that reflects the practice of mounting of the engine at an angle in the frame, first tried in British series production by P & M in their Panther series from the 1930s and which continued to offer vintage-style sloper motorcycles up to 1966.

Sport Tourer
A cross-fertilised of sporty tuning but with comfort additions such as a windshield, padded seat and luggage facilities.

Standard
The 'normal' motorcycle design – upright riding and minimal body fairing or trims.

Superbike
1,000cc class of superb handling motorcycles that have evolved through design innovation over several decades. Emphasis on engineering, handling/suspension, and aerodynamics. Thoroughbred in nature and behaviour.

Touring
A more comfortable motorcycle with specific body design features and engine specifications. Comfortable seating for two. Often highly-faired and chromed. Paint jobs sometimes excessive. Four or six-cylinder low-revving engines.

Velocipede/Early Motorcycle
Very early motorised bicycles pre-1905, that led to 'true' motorcycles circa 1910 and beyond.

Works Scrapper
Not a machine for scrapping on a scrap heap, but a factory racer, often a one-off, designed for fighting or 'scrapping' in races. The most famous such bike being the Brough Company's Superior-based 'Scrapper'.

Engine Types
Key to the culture of the classic motorcycle are the variety of engines used across the century-plus of the motorcycle. Valve, cylinder, and crank design are all crucial, as remains cooling as vital design factor. The core types are:

Single-cylinder: Light, narrow, and simple.

Twin-port single: a more unusual yet efficient head design

Parallel Twin: Light, responsive, good power-to-weight ratio. Crankshaft angle may be more relevant to efficiency in the vertical parallel twin.

Straight-Twin: Narrower, vertical, but longer in the frame.

V-Twin: Low c.g., good torque and cooling. Royal Enfield made the famous KX V-Twin (in-line vertical) in 1936.

Horizontal or 'Boxer' Twin: The flat, low c.g. horizontally opposed engine design also used by some car makers to great effect. Smooth and harmonious but can stick out, and limit roll-angle.

Triple: in-line is a rarer configuration and crucial factor is crankshaft design. Highly efficient. Yamaha XS 750 of note. Triumph triples used counter-balancing shafts.

Triple V-angle: DKW, Honda NS500 and Tait V3 used very unusual single-prone and twin-v-cylinder combination. V3 offers lower c.g. and more cooling passages in head.

In-line Four: High and wider in the frame but very reliable. Good power to weight ratio dependent on engine design.

V-Four: Smooth if well balanced, width depending on v-angle, heavier, but torquey and tuneful.

Flat-Four: Previously popular, as was flat-six. Flat-twins in wider use.

Straight six: In-line type and smooth with primary and secondary internal forces balanced but difficult to mount in a motorcycle frame. BMW 1100cc/1600cc in-line six of note with narrow bores.

V-6: Rare, compact and best known when tried by in-line V6 Laverda endurance bike. A narrow v-angle is beneficial to size and fitting. Narrow-angle VR6 recently tried by old German company Horex (established 1923).

Horizontal Flat Six: Heavy but smooth and powerful, wide in frame, low c.g.

Transverse in-line six: The MV Augusta air-cooled 500cc race bike of 1956 pioneered transverse in-line as a one-off. Latterly, the transverse in-line six was epitomised by Honda RC1666 250cc racer and, the Honda in-line four-derived Benelli Sei 750 transverse six in 1972 as the world's first such road bike engine. Ironically followed by the Honda dohc air-cooled CBX1000 road-going series. Kawasaki Z1300 transverse in-line six was on a grand scale. The transverse in-line six presents conflicts between engine, exhaust and frame requiring solving. Smooth running.

V-8: As seen in the radical Moto Guzzi V, and certain Specials.

Rotary: Rarer is the rotary chambered design, Wankel-type of note. Smooth and light, less vibration and with low c.g. but complex chamber, rotor and tip-sealing and oiling issues inherent.

Above and opposite: Indians old and new. Motorcycling history.

2
THE ART OF THE VISIT

Tips on visiting museums

Harris Mann designed the original Austin Princess, but it was fiddled with by BL. This is the Wolseley version of the wedge on show at the British Motor Museum where essential legends are preserved. (Photo: BMM)

Going to a museum? Then simply turn up, pay the entrance fee and walk or randomly ramble about staring at static exhibits – obvious, is it not? See what you see, know what you knew before you arrived, perhaps glean a new nugget or two from a distance behind a rope, and then leave.

That was the *old* experience of the museum. Things really have changed in the last twenty years or so. We now have a new museum age, and a quick delve into its realisation may help us understand the museum as a new concept and as a philosophy, for that is what museums (including motoring museums) now are, a thought process.

The truth is that if you an enthusiast who wants to make the most of a motor museum, then planning is your best bet. You may think this is too insultingly obvious to discuss, but many people fail to plan their visits and many miss much. It is easily done.

Given how easy it is to access a museum's offering via its website, knowing beforehand what you want to specifically focus on provides a first step in planning your visit. So it is an excellent idea to consider creating a planned, exhibit-by-exhibit schedule. Spontaneity is great, but you can make more of your ticket price and time at a museum by preventing yourself missing a vital 'must see' beforehand. This may seem blindingly obvious to the hardened museum addict, researcher or archivist, but you would be surprised how many knowledgeable motoring enthusiasts miss out on an exhibit or display simply because they were unaware of, or failed to make themselves aware of, a specific exhibit in the time they had during a museum visit.

The new age of museum philosophy

Museums are now about more than the past. They are about new audiences and creating new enthusiasts.

For the reader who is resistant to change, or the reinvention of the museum culture, there is but one question. If we do not educate today's youth into the stories of old cars and old engineering, if we do not seed their minds with what they missed, how will they know and recall, let alone learn, about the century of the automobile, its design and its driving?

Remember, cars have changed massively since the early 1980s. Today's young drive robotised digital devices that convey little of the true meaning of mechanically actuated motoring. They have no idea of how an 'old' car functioned or drove, even a 1980s modern classic.

Young people have to be moved to grasp all this through the motoring museum culture and if that means using new, modern techniques with youth appeal to achieve it, then that is what is needed. Of course, you *can* go too far and create a computer-game of a museum experience that is allegedly 'interactive' as a 'learning experience' and which separates you from actual cars.

'I expected the cars to be more shiny, their paint was poor. And there was no race simulator. We won't go again.'

These are the words of a younger person after visiting a traditional, enthusiast's private collection museum of real cars that were in original, working condition. The expectation was of shiny 'bling' paintwork, digital interaction and of over-restored cars that looked new and perfect. Somehow, this person and people of the same mind set, have to be guided to realising that it is the *story* of a car and its life, its ownership, its patina, that give it its authenticity. Yes, of course, there must be room for the rarefied world of the 'perfect' restored and rescued classic car worth millions as a static exhibit that has been saved for posterity. But weren't cars designed to be driven? It's just a thought . . .

Traditional, unmodernised museums should not be ignored nor dismissed, as they can still deliver a true experience, but they also need to be able to survive. If they remain static in their offering, , they will be roped off for ever.

As in so many debates, there is a balance to be achieved that does not ruin either end of the experience. Visitor numbers and funding may suffer. Somehow a new path is needed, without throwing the baby out with the bath water.

Perhaps above all, in recent years museums have become places of education or 'learning resources' as modern-speak would term it. But the fact is that the old days of exhibiting something old because it is, and expecting people to turn up and stare at it, are over. We now have museum professionals, and a new high art of the museum itself, let alone engagement and interaction with its contents.

Brief visits to museums have been replaced by more in-depth experiences. New theories have been brought to the museum and its creation and operation. Interpretative programmes communicate far better with visitors than static stands to stare at, yet static displays *can* be magical. Museum visitors need to be able to better connect with what they are seeing and what it means as a story. Yet the need for *authenticity* in a museum – especially a motoring museum – must be paramount. All that is 'new' in conceptual terms may not always be entirely appropriate.

Hidden gems of old-fashioned personal collections, devoid of the 'new' museum culture, can still entrance and embrace the old-car enthusiasts and the younger person interested in real, old cars. Here lies a diversity and, a divergence from academic 'new-era' museum thinking. Private museums may straddle the concepts. There has never been a more exciting time in the motoring museum world.

Unlike an historic house museum, a motoring museum focuses in the main on the contents rather than on the structure that houses the contents.

However, many motoring museums also have a remit to make the most of the buildings, old or new, that house them. The whole experience has become vital to the museum visit and yet, the true joy of sheds, converted barns and old buildings, *can* still offer a truly touching and authentic experience to the motoring enthusiast. In our new world of motoring museums, it seems we can touch two worlds that are poles apart, yet which share a love of all things mechanical. As example of this theory, Glasgow's Hadid-designed transport museum is amazing, but so too are the small, men-in-sheds affairs of barns and industrial buildings that populate Britain's museum ranks and many small towns scattered across the world.

As Professor George E. Hein, America's high-priest of museum and active science, has suggested, the new age of the museum is about adapting to a new mechanism and then constructing a new environment to create new thinking in the recipient (the visitor) via the 'constructive museum'. Therein the museum can lead the visitor to make new links between the old and the new. The focus is on the visitor and his or her involvement with and reaction to, what they see and experience, not just on the static event of the exhibition. So were framed the theories of the new museum experience and a new era amid its communication via exhibition and learning in museums. It is a theory of education, now applied to museums and those of us who visit them and immerse ourselves in the new age of the museum experience.

Put simply, many 'old' museums were often deliverers of set, systematic, traditional, ordered thinking, whereas the 'new' museum provides the visitor with a new journey, a new mechanism of discovery and self- constructed knowledge. Some museums have blended the two poles of museum practice and it seems to work. Making cars work, and driving working cars, is also vital.

Yet people who know what they like and do not want to know what they don't – where they refuse to see or view anything outside their known norms – are more difficult for the museum to educate. Perceived wisdom can be a contradiction in terms, a barrier to learning when visiting a museum. So the new world of the museum is to think laterally.

Museums do not now just present a static interpretation of the past, but instead provide a modern translation of a past into a more 'real' and far more accessible and engaging process of exhibition. Again, in plain English, the role of the museum is no longer to trickle-feed the passive mind looking for a momentary reaction, but to provoke new thoughts in a more active engagement. And again, if today's youth have never driven a 'real' pre-digital car, then should not a museum encourage them to do just that, to drive a 'proper' mechanical car not a computerised authoritarian 'thing' where the commander ends up asking 'what's it doing now?'

Above: In search of Petroliana: Old cans are now big business.

Left: Gilera delights at a private motorcycle museum.

The museum as thought provocation

The respected museum academic Eilean Hooper-Greenhill had it right when she framed the new educational role of the museum in a new age of communication, and engagement; the 'provocation' of making the museum visitor think about the museum and its contents, and the engagement with them, in a new way. As Hooper-Greenhill suggested, what were once seen as 'the general public' by museums, are now seen as the 'active audience', which surely opens many doors to new experiences. In today's museums, old and young people can engage and interact with exhibits and mechanisms in a new way. But surely, we should beware the total take-over of the boxed-in display and the digital and interactive 'exhibit station'?

Self-instruction during a museum visit is still possible, but the role of the museum has changed dramatically in the last two decades or so. The results of the change can be experienced in making the most of the art of the visit. And in a museum, do we learn by input and learned behavioural response, or do we learn through stimulation and then searching for more, or do we learn though the blending of such processes? It all depends on what type of person you are and what you are looking for in a museum. All this is as true in motoring museum as it is a major art museum. And anyway, cars *are* art!

The twenty-first century museum has become so much more than a museum as we once perceived the museum to be. The static, the solely visual, have been evolved into a museum narrative, on-site activities, interaction, and far beyond into education, community and club engagement. That is why car clubs and events are now vital at museums. The motoring museum visit has become a social event and a drivers' gathering. Car restoration can also be watched as it happens. This can only be a good thing, not least to inspire youth to drive and fettle 'real' cars.

Above all this lies the new art of museum-making and management. It seems to work – given the rise of the museum and its new culture.

As motoring enthusiasts, we need to recognise this and to support museums. If you have ever wondered why modern museums are so good, so different from what went before, the new museum culture and the philosophy behind it (as briefly cited above), provides you with the explanation. If you keep going back to a museum, then you know that that museum has succeeded in its constructive mission – why else would you return?

Time is the other big factor in a museum visit, especially when it you are visiting a massive museum with many floors, halls, displays and separate collections in adjoining buildings. Indeed, two-day visits with local overnight accommodation packages seem to be the ideal for answer for visiting the larger museums. The best advice for one-day visits is, arrive early, stop for lunch, and leave late! Again, to make the most of a museum visit, it is about the art of planning ahead.

Paying extra for a museum guide is probably worthwhile if you are a car club or small group of enthusiasts – divided up, the fee is either a small extra, or free,

and with an expert on hand, a visit can be truly enhanced. A recent visit to the superb Brunel/SS *Great Britain* museum in Bristol with my car club, saw an 'old-hand' of a Brunel expert provided for an accompanied tour and his knowledge significantly added to the experience of the art of the visit.

We can assume that museums have provided for the disabled, the visually or hearing impaired, or those requiring other assistance. What we should not assume is that museums should answer detailed historical research questions for free – and on the spur of the moment. Many museums do operate a professional archive and research service and quite correctly charge a fee for access to their libraries and material. Again, speaking to the correct person and making an appointment prior to your visit and being aware of the fees is the sensible path to research for the motoring enthusiast and historian. And if you expect such services for free – then many might ask why?

As example, there are 10,000-plus books in the National Motor Museum library; they need securing, housing, caring for and someone employed to run the library. Why would you expect such a facility to exist free of charge in an age of huge costs, health and safety edicts and increasing value?

Rare Citroën mascot on a Traction Avant convertible. Such mascots are also a museum sub-culture.

Many museums provide an archive or historical service and some even run courses for budding historians and writers. Gloves should be worn and permits sought for archival investigations. For the true enthusiast, these archives are well worth attending. Check for details with the museum via its website or a through a telephone call. Do not turn up at a museum and expect to be told where your grandfather's car, last seen in 1959, is! Sounds incredible? It happens, often, as do requests to date and value mundane machinery and not-so-special memorabilia and photographs. The *Antiques Roadshow* has got a lot to answer for.

Restoring cars does not come cheap and often exceeds the actual value of the more mundane vehicle. Yet barn find and scrap heap restorations are

now carried out by museums at vast expense – adding to the costs of creating a museum and employing people within it.

'Running Days' – be they petrol or steam, club events, marque celebrations, and re-enactments of days gone by – are the very stuff of museums. A brilliant idea is that of allowing enthusiasts to ride classic motorcycles at the UK's National Motorcycle Museum. For a rational fee, you can join up as 'Friend' and get the chance to ride old motorcycles on site under the guidance of an expert; what a great way to relive your past in a safe and sensible manner that helps perpetuate a museum. If anything captures the art of the visit, then this surely does.

Indeed, becoming a 'Friend' of a museum or a trust is a great way of offering your support, making a commitment and receiving enhanced benefits; this may be the new way to go.

It is hard to forget vintage Bugatti days at Prescott, a 'vintagent' day, or the re-opening of the newly restored original start-finish straight at Brooklands when thousands of true enthusiasts turned out to lean against the fence to see old cars in noisy and smelly action – as they were intended to perform.

Across Europe, America, Australia and beyond there are now dedicated museum tours, driving days, and museum-by-museum visits by car clubs as part of the 'touring' events. A World Forum of Motor Museums exists, as does the Australasian Motor Museum Association.

Museums have responded with better facilities, new exhibits and much more, notably multi-million pound investments, advanced architecture, virtual displays and stunning cars, and in doing so, have upgraded the world of the motor museum. But they need to be careful that they do not isolate the car and the visitor from the story of motoring, of mechanical engineering and design.

Static exhibits are superb, but nothing adds to a museum as much as 'running' of engines or chassis and the tangible reality of combusted fuel, whirring magnetos, cars, motorcycles, and buses careering about, and owners fettling 'live' machines under open, access-for-all conditions. Such days are held regularly at our motor museums and we should encourage museum operators to hold as many as possible for all things wheeled, and winged.

Money

Museums are special places, run by great people and dedicated enthusiasts, often with private funding at the patronage of the owners. One thing is for sure, we owe a lot to the people who have founded and funded our car museums and trusts.

Surely it is correct that we should enjoy and support our motor museums, whatever their size, wherever they may be. Things have a come a long way in the world of the motor museum and we have benefactors, directors, general managers

and all the paid and non-paid voluntary staff to thank for such memories. For the art of the museum in its new age is now upon us; perhaps we should reply with the refining the art of the museum visit?

Above all, we should remember that many museums and their exhibits are private, or charity or trust owned, and need money to open, operate, employ, and survive. How do you think it all happens? Not by magic, but by money, and by kindness. Museums should be fun, exciting, stimulating and both a learning experience and an emotional experience. But should they exist in a preserved past? Of course not.

If we expect excellence then surely we must be prepared to pay for it? The argument some people make for the 'free-to-enter' museum is not invalid in certain specific contexts of national setting, but if you expect our *motoring* past to survive, then proper funding is vital. After all, look where limited and argued-about State-funding and ill-conceived partial privatisation (PFI) under the politics of *both* the

Bugatti on the move. Paul Tebbett's Bugatti beauty caught as it leaves Prescott on a late evening.

Allardette, the supercharged Ford Anglia, part of a private collection.

main political parties got the National Health Service in all its continuing crises. Museum policy and funding is a national issue and so very vital to our learning. Imagine a child denied museums (or libraries)!

Snap-happy?

Photography is a key area of concern for visitors and for museums themselves. Private photography on your visit will mostly be not just allowed, but encouraged, yet dropped cameras denting cars, or cameras, bags, or straps, scratching cars on display is a common and regrettable factor in museum life. It is so easy to dent or scratch a valuable car, and this is why so many are roped off – much to the annoyance of some visitors who want to get a better shot. Yet the truth is that the bills for rectification work can be enormous. The visitor should surely have self-awareness and make a conscious effort to avoid creating danger with camera, bag, coat, or other items when in close proximity to a car; even a metal stud or zip on an coat can inflict bodywork damage as the wearer manoeuvres up to vehicle. As for a dropped camera on bodywork, this is the big danger. For the non-professional it is simple, ensure that the camera strap is around your neck, or if is a compact camera, around your wrist. Mobile telephones and tablet devices do not have straps, so do not drop them on a car.

Museum photography for commercial, professional and published use has grey areas and definite areas. At least £2million of public liability insurance is often required and a certificate to be seen before a museum will allow you to take professional or commercial use photographs. But if you are on a private visit,

but using an obviously expensively professional quality camera , with undeclared photo sales or website posting in mind, then you enter the grey area of 'private' photography that is not. CCTV in museums will soon have an eagle-eyed museum administrator down to talk you if you are making photography that is clearly something more than a private record. It might be ok to remove a printed notice from the windscreen of a car before you photograph it for yourself, but what if you scratch that car in doing so? Great care is needed when up close and personal with exhibits.

Be it a film crew or a professional or semi-professional photographer, people cannot just turn up and 'expect' or see as a 'right of admission' the facility to go beyond private recording. If you want to go beyond the expected, private norms with photography or filming, then contact the museum and its relevant person *before* your visit.

For the private visitor and photographer, many museums do of course want to encourage your visit, but the museums have a simple and not unreasonable request: please show the exhibits the respect you would expect for your own personal property; reading the terms and conditions of entry might not be such a bad idea.

Museums endeavour to provide us with evidence as to why we should saviour our museums and what they do, and plan the art of our visit. We should surely make our museums special.

3

MUSEUM-BY-MUSEUM

L isted below are nearly 100 British motoring, motorcycle and transport museums including commercial, bus and truck museums. A full listing of global transport museums (over 400+) is included in this book and so too are brief out-takes from visits to selected overseas museums (see chapter 4).

We start by heading west to Bristol where great British airliners and great British cars were once made at Filton, home of our first museum entry. The Brunel story is also told in Bristol down on the harbour. The Oakham Treasures Tractor & Farm Museum is just up the road at Portbury. About a 20 minute drive north up the road from Bristol can be found Gloucester, its museums and the place where aircraft (note, Museum of the Jet Age) and the Cotton motorcycle were manufactured. The Classic Motor Hub at Bibury is also nearby and well worth the trip.

  The Bugatti Trust and museum at Prescott is 40 minutes' drive north of Bristol, and the Haynes International Museum is 80 minutes' drive south. The Atwell-Wilson Museum at Calne is an hour's drive south east. The National Motor Museum at Beaulieu is two hour's drive south, and the Cotswold Motoring Museum and Toy Collection at Bourton-on-the-Water is 50 minutes' drive north east. The Steam Museum (railway-focused) at Swindon is an hour east. Cardiff and its national museum is an hour west. Swansea's bus museum is that way too. The Aston Martin Heritage Trust at Wallingford is 100 minutes east. The British Motor Museum at Gaydon is two hours north west via the M6.

  Just up the road from the British Motor Museum, at Coventry University can be found the Lanchester Museum and its library and interactive archive telling the story of Sir Frederick Lanchester, the engineer known as Britain's 'Leonardo da Vinci' due to his stunning future-vision of design and invention.

MOTOR MUSEUMS A-Z GUIDE

AEROSPACE BRISTOL

(Incorporating the Bristol Aero Collection/Bristol Car Company Collection)
Hayes Way, Patchway
Bristol BS34 5BZ
Telephone: 01179 315 315
Opening hours: 1000-1700 seven days a week until 1 November. Check for Winter hours.
www.aerospacebristol.org

Here can be found a wonderful mix of old and less old. As a headline act, Concorde is displayed in a stunning setting that truly captures its magic and our loss. Close by can be found arrayed the history and output of the Bristol Aeroplane Company – as aircraft and cars (Bristol Car Division/Bristol Cars) under the aegis of the Bristol Aero Collection Trust. The Bristol Owners Heritage Trust contributes to the collection and helps ensure that the cars of their marque remain appreciated by those in the know, and a wider audience.

Concorde is the key here, but 'Bristol' cars and engineering are to the fore amid many displays.

Located in a new home, the gems of Bristol aero and auto production can be seen, although much is now hidden from view, being in store, in comparison to the previous Kemble airfield facility. Nevertheless, this new museum is a superb day out and worthy of a day's study. If only the Bristol Britannia currently sited at Kemble could be moved to this new museum site.

From its beginning as the Bristol and Colonial Aeroplane Company, through to the Bristol 401 car and its subsequent models into the millennium, including the Bristol racing team, this is a great story superbly told at a state-of the art museum facility that deserves its status. From Bristol cars and airliners such as the Brabazon, the Britannia, and beyond, there are many stories on show here at Filton – the Bristol Company's old home and Concorde's last redoubt where many emotions are expressed. What we once did and what we have lost is painfully obvious here, even if Brits do built Airbus wings nearby.

This is a top class museum that does the city and its marque proud, but we might regret the high price of eating-in at the museum cafe. My car club had a great time here and many clubs are congregating at this venue, often during a driving tour. There is plenty of parking and several hours of interest.

Although Hangar 15 does show off archive and artefacts, including a 1953 Bristol 403, perhaps more room can be found for displaying more of the Bristol Aero Collection archives and store. Enthusiasts seem to think this would be good. Sacrificing a bit of architect-designed glossy floor space for an oily rag parts and memorabilia display would add charm and character, surely? Despite such caveats, this is a stunner of a museum and already a revered shrine highly recommended by many.

AMBERLEY MUSEUM & HERITAGE CENTRE

Houghton Bridge, Arundel,
West Sussex, BN18 9L
Telephone: 01798 831370
Opening hours: Wednesdays to Sundays 10.00 -1630. Note: Winter season alterations.
www.amberley,musuem.co.uk

Although not strictly a motoring museum, this *is* a transport and heritage museum and has the added attraction of being set on a 36 acre site in the South Downs National Park. The museum's principal transport-related attraction is a collection of local, historic buses (Southdown), some owned by the museum and others on permanent loan to the museum.

Dedicated to the industrial heritage of the South East, the museum also include a narrow-gauge railway and a bus service (both provide free nostalgic travel around the site). Exhibits and displays include: 'Connected Earth'; Telecommunications Hall; Milne Electricity Hall; Printing Workshop. Regular vintage and classic car events are held here.

If you are interested in buses – of a specific locality – then this is a museum to visit.

ANGLESEY TRANSPORT MUSEUM

Tacla Taid Transport and Agriculture Museum,
Tyddyn Pwrpas, Newborough,
Anglesey, LL61 6TN.
Telephone: 01248 440344
Opening hours:1000-1700 March-October
www.angleseytransportmuseum.com

This museum is packed with over 100 vintage cars, classic motorcycles, military vehicles, and farm machinery dating back as far as the 1920s. The museum was started by a Welsh lorry driver's son, Arfon Williams; he often accompanied his father on long runs and grew up with a love for all forms of transport. Today he is the owner of Ty Crwn Garage at Gaerwen, one of the largest privately owned garages on Anglesey.

Opened 32 years ago, the garage has metamorphosed into a working restoration centre and the linked museum. In April, 2001, Arfon opened the Anglesey Transport and Agriculture Museum, the largest museum of its kind in Wales. Of note, the Land-Rover marque is highlighted at the garage and the museum.

Although a long way west, this museum is interesting, different, and well worth a visit from the true enthusiast, with hours of fun and learning to be had here.

ANSON ENGINE MUSEUM

Anson Rd, Poynton,
Cheshire
SK12 1TD.
Opening hours:
Telephone: 01625 874 426
Open on Friday's 1000-1600 and open one 'steaming' weekend a month from Easter until end of October. See website for updates.
wwwenginemuseum.org

Situated just south of Manchester on the site of the old Anson Colliery, this is the place to revel in static engines of many types. The engine-focused museum is the outcome of years of work, restoration and collecting by two enthusiasts – Les Cawley and Geoff Challinor.

The museum is a registered charity and does not receive government funding. To date most of the work has been carried out and funded by the volunteers and Friends of the museum. It was described by one of its visitors as 'run on a shoestring and fuelled by enthusiasm'.

The museum now houses a unique collection of over 250 gas and oil engines, many maintained in running order, ranging from early Crossley gas engines through to more modern diesels. Engine enthusiasts from all over the world come to visit this fascinating museum. The Les & Ena Cawley Memorial Building is home to a fantastic display showing the development of the internal combustion engine. The museum has secured many early examples from other major museums including the Science Museum and museums in Edinburgh, Birmingham & Bristol.

Displays include a steam section with two Robey engines; an A frame and a beam engine. Pride of place goes to the Stott engine that used to drive a cotton wadding mill in Hazel Grove. It was rescued by the museum and has been lovingly restored to working condition by the volunteers. It ran in 2011 for the first time in over 50 years.

Engines run every day the museum is open, and every month engines in the steam section can be found 'in steam'. A blacksmith, bodger, collier and wood turner display also adds authenticity to this great, niche offering in the world of static engines. To hear the engines whirring, popping, breathing, wheezing and rattling amid the smell of combustion is a great sensory experience for the mechanical motor enthusiast.

Exhibits of gas, oil, and steam engines include:

Largest running Crossley Atmospheric engine ever made
Mirrlees No 1 – 1st diesel engine built in UK
Gardner 4T5
Furnival engine running printing press
National engine running a typical workshop
Giant model of Poynton showing collieries around the area
Range of rare static engines dating back 100 years

ASTON MARTIN HERITAGE TRUST

Drayton St. Leonard,
Wallingford,
Oxfordshire, OX10 7BG, UK.
Telephone: 01865-400414
Museum Hours: Monday to Friday, 1st & 3rd Saturday of each month. 1000-1630. Closed Bank Holidays.
Email: Curator@amht.org.uk
Website: www.amht.org.uk

This is a small, but intimate and up-close Aston Martin experience that seems to be aimed at the knowledgeable marque enthusiast, and those of a wider motoring interest, although any member of the interested public is clearly welcome. It is an excellent offering.

Founded in 1998, the Trust opened its Museum and Archive in 2002 in the historic tithe barn at Drayton St Leonard in Oxfordshire, UK. The Trust is also the official archive for Aston Martin Lagonda Ltd., and for the Aston Martin Owners Club.

Some people might perceive Aston Martin in the more modern contexts of its varied ownerships and existences – James Bond has got a lot to answer for. However, the truth is that Aston Martin reaches back to the months before the First World War in 1914 when

Lionel Martin and Robert Bamford built a series of tuned -up engines, and a prototype chassis based on an Isotta-Frashini provenance. The first true Aston Martin branded cars were created from 1922, although various 'one-offs' and 'Specials' make earlier claims. Having been wound-up, then restarted in 1925 with A.C. Bertelli as chief engineer/ designer, Aston Martin went on to great things and made noteworthy appearances at Le Mans as early as 1932 and 1932. Aston Martin has been through many incarnations since, yet survives, as do its values and vital ingredients. The significant achievements of the 'Gauntlett' years are not to be overlooked amid the many incarnations of Aston Martin that range from AML, David Brown, and Ford relationships.

The museum Trust has a very significant and growing collection of original items relating to all aspects of the Aston Martin marque, which is secured for future generations. A dedicated team of unpaid volunteers and Trustees supports a small number of professional staff in caring for the collections and the visitors. The Aston Martin Heritage Trust Collections Catalogue is now digitised.

A range of cars and Aston Martin artefacts are displayed in the wonderful environs of the medieval barn and include:

Aston Martin 'A3' is the earliest surviving Aston Martin in the world. The third 'true' Aston Martin ever made, this is a very important part of Aston Martin history. 'A3', using the early side-valve engine, and rather flexible chassis, first saw the light of day in 1921. It had a very active early life as a prototype, demonstrator and racer.

Aston Martin Ulster K4/508/U was transferred into the care and ownership of the Aston Martin Heritage Trust in 1998, this rare 1934 Ulster is one of only four 2/4 seat cars among the 21 production Ulsters made. It was owned up until his death in 1974 by Lewis Treece, at which time it was bequeathed to the Club. The 1495cc engined tourer is kept in roadworthy, mechanical order and road registered. It can often be seen at AMHT/AMOC events.

Aston Martin V12 Vanquish Cutaway 2000

Aston Martin Vanquish Volante 2014

Aston Martin AM Vantage Nimrod – NRAC2/004

Aston Martin One-77 Design Verification Model

Note: Due to the barn's space constrictions, changes to the choice of cars exhibited at any one time can mean that the cars on show can change dependent on choice by the Trust. See website for current updates.

ATWELL-WILSON MOTOR MUSEUM

Downside, Stockley Lane, Calne,
Wiltshire, SN11 0NF.
Telephone: 01249 813119
Opening: During the summer (throughout April to October) the museum is open
Tuesday-Sunday inclusive 1100-1700 and bank holidays.
Off season opening hours (throughout November, February and March) are
Thursday-Sunday inclusive 1100-1600
Winter opening hours (throughout December and January, except Christmas Day
when the museum is closed) are Saturday and Sunday 1100-1600
Website: www.atwellwilson.org.uk

Although it might be small, this museum is crammed with motoring memorabilia,
automotive artefacts, a diverse range of cars, motorcycles, toys, and has over
100 wheeled exhibits. Originally known as the Downside Collection, the story
was started by Richard and Hasell Atwell and run by them until their passing; the
majority of the exhibits are cars from the 1920s onwards and include founding
exhibits such as: 1937 Buick Albermarle, 1934 Vauxhall 14/6, and 1931 Singer
Junior. A 1930s Buick that drove 150,000 miles in the tropics under the command
of its sugar magnate owner (Tate and Lyle) is a rare beast indeed. So too is a
'perfect' last-off-the-line Rover SD1 Vitesse Twin Plenum.

Now run as a charity, this place is a true gem of that wonderful thing – the
small, hidden, museum. You could probably get around the exhibits in an hour,
but a proper inspection and a proper wallow in nostalgia, means that two to
three hours can easily pass by. The staff are all volunteers and have interesting
backgrounds – including in the engineering and aerospace industries. These
volunteers are a fund of old-timer knowledge.

A rare and valuable collection of original large-scale aircraft 'models' of
1920s-1950s aircraft hangs from the ceiling.

Several halls and a new 'shed' provide an eclectic and excellent range of cars
from early motoring to modern classics. An FSO Polonez rubs shoulders with
Riley RM series cars, Austin Sevens. Here, the last off the line Triumph Dolomite
Sprint vies with an Issigonis Mini 9x 'gearless' prototype (Issigonis' own car in
fact), Saab 99, Opel Manta, early Toyota Celica fastback (the Mustang 'copy'),
old MGs and Rovers, and rare Ford, Trojan, and BL fare. Some unusual American
cars lurk in the halls, as does an automatic Morris Ital 1300, and an electric
Peugeot 106. Jaguars are evident, and so too is something very rare indeed – the
1960s MGB 'lookalike' that was the 1967 Datsun Fairlady1500 roadster that
was originally purchased new, by no less than the Standard Motor Company, for
secret evaluation.

A 1924 Brough Superior of family ownership provenance and reputedly in original specification and content, is a rare and wonderful thing. Ariel, BSA and Triumph motorcycles are all on show amid over twenty two-wheeled exhibits, including a 1972 Russian, Voskhod twin port single.

The collection of motorcycles, mopeds and bicycles is complemented by interesting memorabilia, the Jack Spittle Model Collection, and the 'Jack French' reconstructed 1930s style garage complete with vehicles. Jack French was a famed 'specials' builder and racer with Austin Seven-based Formula profile – a 'garagiste' 750 Motor Club racer who was famous in his day. The rare and unique one-off Dodge-engined Allard K-Type 'Red Ram' was resident at the museum after its return from South America and has now passed to a new owner in Germany. Several 'interesting' cars remain on loan to the museum from owners and from the British Motor Museum at Gaydon.

In 1981, the collection was brought together under one roof with the completion of the smallest of the three buildings. Following the construction in 1989 of what is now the Main Hall, the Museum as it is today was forged. In 1997, a Charitable Trust was formed to take over the operation of the Museum, followed shortly by the formulation of a support group of volunteers as 'The Friends'.

The most recent expansion occurred in 2003 with the aid of a grant from the Heritage Lottery Fund. After the deaths of Richard and Hasell Atwell as founders, the present Charity basis was formed in 1997.

Secreted away in rural Wiltshire, this is a charming and authentic museum that caters for knowledgeable enthusiasts, 'oldies', and also for family visitors and youngsters who want to learn. It is typical of a traditional British motor museum that has cleverly adapted with the times yet not lost its soul or small town charm. Small, intimate, characterful, non-digital and an utterly authentic gem, all this museum needs is the serving of refreshments and it would be perfect. Recommended for the enthusiast and do ask to see the workshop.

Motorcycles of note at Atwell Wilson:

1923 Raleigh 14 250cc
1924 Douglas 2¾
1924 Brough Superior
1939 Ariel Square 4G
1954 BSA 500cc Goldstar
1956 Triumph 650cc Trophy
1957 BSA red Rocket
1958 Ariel Square 4/2

1963 Triumph Bonneville 650
1972 Voskhod Twin Port Single
1978 Mobylette Master
1980 Honda CB125

BATTLESBRIDGE MOTORCYCLE MUSEUM

Battlesbridge Antiques Centre, Battlesbridge,
Chelmsford, Essex.
Opening times: Sunday 1100-1600
www.battlesbridge.co.uk

This small museum has a motorcycle memorabilia collection of interest. Only open on Sundays, the venue is small and yet interesting and the collection is ideal for motorcycle enthusiasts.

BEAMISH MUSEUM

Beamish,
County Durham,
DH9 0RG.
Telephone 0191 370 4000
Open daily (except some national holidays) 1000-1600.
Winter hours: February-April. Summer Hours April to November.
www.beamish.org.uk

Beamish was the vision of Dr Frank Atkinson, the Museum's founder and first director. It has recently received a £10million Lottery grant.

Frank had visited Scandinavian folk museums in the early 1950s and was inspired to create an open air museum for the North East. He realised that the region was losing its industrial heritage. Coal mining, ship building and iron and steel manufacturing were disappearing, along with the communities that served them.

By 1958, Frank wanted the new museum to illustrate the way of life of ordinary people and bring the region's history alive. 22 ex-Army surplus wooden huts formed the basis of this intriguing museum. Today, a rebuilt and expanded Beamish remains true to Frank's principles today and brings history to life for hundreds of thousands of visitors each year.

Industrial engines, artefacts, cars, engines, lorries and all manner of industry-related items can be found at this diverse museum that caters for a range of interests and which many recommend.

BENTLEY (W.O.) MEMORIAL FOUNDATION

Foundation Building,
Ironstone Lane,
Wroxton, Banbury OX15 6ED, UK.
www.wobmf.co.uk

A small museum, archive and library dedicated to W.O. Bentley. Opened in 2006. Home to the Bentley Drivers Club. Open to members and the public by appointment only.

BETWS-Y-COED MOTOR MUSEUM

Station Road,
Gwynedd, LL24 0AH
Opening hours; 1030-1730 daily Easter to end of October.
Telephone 01690 710760

Small but perfectly formed as they say. An intimate collection that it says is 'unique'. At £2.00, the admission fee is almost unique. Based on the Houghton family private collection, this museum has survived the tide of change and continues towards yet another decade.

It contains approximately 30 cars, these include a rare-bodied, Bugatti T57, the ex-Grosvenor Riley MPH, Aston Martin (Bertelli-bodied), and a range of mainstream marques. A 1927 Standard Stratford Tourer is on show. Morgan three-wheelers with JAP, and Matchless engines were also present. Motorcycles, children's cars, models and memorabilia all on show.

Gloriously unmodernised, an authentic museum in a great setting that is unpretentious and the much-loved work of a family. Well worth supporting and visiting.

BEXHILL MUSEUM

Egerton Road, Bexhill-on-Sea,
East Sussex, TN39 3HL.
Telephone: 01424 222058
www.bexhillmuseum.co.uk

More of local community museum than a motor museum, Bexhill can however offer the specific attraction of a display charting the Elva Mk III car and its racing heritage across six decades. References to Bexhill's position in the early history British road race heritage are also included. There was a Bexhill 'Grand Prix' class race in 1902 and in more recent years a Bexhill Motoring Festival has been held. In 2007, the actor Eddie Izzard became this museum's patron. Unusual in its motoring content for a local community museum, Bexhill is lesser known but well worth a visit.

BICESTER HERITAGE / BICESTER MOTION

Buckingham Road,
Bicester,
Oxfordshire, OX27 8AL,UK.
Telephone: 01869 327928
Opening hours and events – see website as they vary
www.bicesterheritage.co.uk

Bicester Heritage, set on a near-350 acre site, is the new age of niche enthusiasm that combines business with preservation, and restoration amid a living, viable culture of motoring, mechanical and museum themes. Daniel Geoghegan is the man who began this lateral thinking reinvention from 2013 as a modern 'hub'. Today it forges ahead with a diverse range of inhabitants and events and a five-year plan for expansion and now part of 'Bicester Motion' as an over-arching brand and mechanism for the expansion of this hub concept.

Bicester Heritage is creating a revolution in historic vehicle ownership. The unique location is the UK's only hub for historic motoring excellence and is a national centre for all things mechanical.

It has gone from a standing start to a home for over 30 specialist businesses with a collective turnover of over £20m. Although it might be best to attend on specific event days, however many of the businesses are open daily and the likes of Historit are typical of the enthusiasm shown inside the old car world. Car dealers, restorers, collections, and experts are all housed here. Appointments to view may be required, but if you are a true and knowledgeable enthusiast, many of the on-site businesses are happy to grant access, provided you are of classic car ilk and know how to behave around valuable cars. Who knows, you might purchase a car here!

Bicester Scramble Days have become legends in a very short time, as has the Classic and Sports Car Show in association with Flywheel. This presents visitors with an eclectic mix of vintage cars, aircraft and military machinery, much of it moving and working. The atmosphere at a Bicester all-action day is tangible and

of the right cars and the right crowd of old and of today. Bicester can only be called brilliant. We can only hope that ticket prices do not become stratospheric in the current fashionable mode for 'special' or VIP events.

BIGGAR ALBION FOUNDATION/MUSEUM

BAF.
19 North Back Road,
Biggar,
ML12 6EJ,
Lanarkshire
Scotland,
biggaralbion.org.uk

At time of writing this trust is fundraising to secure a move to a new location amid a new museum set-up. Intended re-opening is cited as 2019. It is still active and still holding its annual classic vehicle rally. The foundation was an offshoot of the Biggar Museum Trust and dedicated to the preservation of the Scottish, Albion marque – Albion motor car company – and commercial vehicle manufacturer.

Now into its fifth decade, the Albion preservation movement has a large following and holds many vehicles and artefacts in preservation across its membership and own stock. Albion was established in Glasgow in 1899 and was known the world over for its engineering standards – almost ship built!

The Biggar Albion Foundation Ltd has a dozen or so Albion vehicles and has reportedly secured a new home at the Gladstone Court Museum site in Biggar – close to the Foundation's own premises at North Back Road. The museum has been open since 1993. Commercial vehicle/lorry fans should not have to wait too long for the marque to reassert its heritage status in an active new museum.

BIRMINGHAM SCIENCE MUSEUM 'THINKTANK'

Millennium Point,
Curzon Street, Digbeth,
Birmingham, UK.
www.birminghammuseums.org.uk/thinktank

Birmingham Science Museum (formerly known as just as Thinktank) is a museum of science, engineering and rebranded amid a technology framework – with wider

appeal to the public. Opened in 2001, it is part of Birmingham Museums Trust and is located within the Millennium Point complex. It had an impressive 230,830 visitors in 2017.

The Birmingham Collection of Science & Industry was started in the mid-nineteenth century, initially consisting of collections of weapons from the gun trade and the Birmingham Proof House. The Birmingham Museum & Art Gallery opened in 1885, including science collections. In 1951, the Museum of Science and Industry opened at Elkington Silver Electroplating Works, Newhall Street. Over the following years, the museum acquired individual artefacts, as well as entire collections, that were related to local industry and the history of science and technology. By the 1990s, the museum had become known as the Birmingham Science Museum, but it had cars in its collection – how could it not?

This former museum closed in 1997 and with new funding, the 'Thinktank' branded museum operation opened on 29 September 2001 as part of the £114-million Millennium Point complex. While many objects were put on display at Thinktank, others were stored at the Birmingham Museum Collection Centre.

In March 2015, a new 'Spitfire gallery' opened, relating the displayed aircraft to their production locally and one of around 10,000 Spitfires that were manufactured at Castle Bromwich, is displayed.

Exhibits include:

Mercedes Benz car licence manufactured by Star Motor Company, Wolverhampton, in 1898, given to the museum in 1965.

Lanchester Petrol Electric Motorcar. Designed and manufactured by Sir Frederick William Lanchester in 1926.

Austin Seven Austin Seven Tourer car, Registration number XO 4133. Built in 1923, owned by the factory until 1944 before passing to private ownership. It is the ninth oldest example of the 300 remaining.

Morris Mini-Minor Registration number XEW 583, built in 1959.

BO'NESS MOTOR MUSEUM

Bridgeness Road,
Bo'ness,
Falkirk,
EH51 9JR
Scotland.

Telephone: 01506 827007
Opening hours: 1000-1600 daily/seasonal/
www.bonessmotormuseum.co.uk

On the coast, close to the site of the old Bo'ness circuit, Bo'ness is small and
niche museum to visit. First thought of by Colin Anderson in 1999, it contains a
small gathering of 25 or so classic cars – from a 2CV, a James Bond BMW 750,
to a Ford Anglia, and a range of TV and film cars and props (not all are original
however). This includes a 'Return of the Saint', white Jaguar XJ-S Mk1 and a
Lotus Esprit film prop car.

The museum has always had a James Bond selection, including Aston Martin
exhibits and Bond ephemera. Older classic car owners might expect to see more about
the Bo'ness circuit and its competition history, but this is still a good little museum if
one of singular context and character that reflects its owner's passions. Not a forensic,
classic car marque museum experience, but a successful smaller museum.

BRITISH COMMERCIAL VEHICLE MUSEUM

King Street,
Leyland,
Preston, Lancashire .
PR25 2LE
Telephone: 01772 451011
Opening hours: 1000-1630 Tuesday-Sunday
www.britishcommercialvehcilemuseum.com

Billed as one of the 'finest motor museums in Europe' – which is no mean claim –
this museum of the truck, lorry, camion and commercial certainly packs a punch.

Moored up on an old Leyland Motors site, there are 60 vehicles displayed, some
dating back over 120 years. Not much is roped off, and there a superb collections
of related ephemera/memorabilia. Steam wagons, lorries, fire engines, buses, they
are all here. A 1922 12hp Star and an early Leyland Tiger, add to the aura. Access
is also allowed on-board the vehicles, which is a very good thing.

The Chairman of the museum's Trustees is John Gilchrist, who used to be
Chairman and Chief Executive of Leyland Trucks. Enough said – talk about
grabbing the right man.

The museum boasts a substantial archive of historic importance, covering
Leyland Vehicles, Albion, AEC, Scammell, Guy, as well as general transport,
technical, engineering, design, and manufacturing subjects.

We might suggest that this is a true 'sensory' experience in new-museum culture, but thankfully it has not got too carried away with 'new-museum age' electrickery. Recently refurbished, and with an excellent cafe that serves proper food and drinks, this place is also family friendly, although expect to see quite a few old codgers in flat caps reminiscing upon past glories, and why not, they deserve to.

Winner of a Visit England 'Hidden Gem' award in 2014, this is indeed an excellent museum. Even if commercials are not your special interest, there is much to be seen and learned here. Highly recommended and a top tier museum that deserves not be ignored amid the classic car fever and car-museum focus. As a local said of the museum, 'Trucking brilliant.'

BRITISH MOTOR MUSEUM

Banbury Road, Gaydon, Warwickshire,
CV35 0BJ.
Open 1000-1700 daily.
Location: Adjacent to Junction 12 M40 Motorway on B4100.
Telephone: 01926 64118
Website: britishmotormuseum.co.uk

Above all, the sheer scope of the BMC, BL, and British marques displayed never fails to impress. For fans of the best and less-than-best years of British car making, this museum is *the* location and resource. As a motoring museum, irrespective of its BL marque affiliation, it ranks as world-class and hugely authentic in the experience.

Formerly known as the Heritage Motor Centre, the museum is situated in Gaydon, Warwickshire, just off junction 12 of the M40. The Museum building is itself a spectacular piece of architecture with an Art Deco design, whilst the active, mechanically busy 'Collections Centre' building is a modern contrast.

This major national museum opened in 1993 as the amalgamation of the British Motor Industry Heritage Trust's preserved car collection. The Trust decided that the car collection and artefacts were outgrowing its then two locations, Studley in Warwickshire and the museum in Syon Park in West London – better known in the past as the 'Heritage Collection London'.

From the Studley Castle outbuildings – home to BL Heritage Ltd as home to a 'Leyland Historic Vehicles' collection, the collection had matured into a Trust as they had outgrown its accommodation at the Longbridge factory. In 1978, the archive collections and vehicle workshop moved to Studley Castle which British Leyland had acquired in the 1970s as a conference and training facility.

Some vehicles had been put on display at Donington Park but, at the end of 1980, a larger selection moved to a small museum in the grounds of Syon Park in London.

In 1983, the British Motor Industry Heritage Trust (BMIHT) was formed to secure the collection for the Nation. The BMIHT owns a wide range of historical items which help describe the long and varied history of motor car manufacture in Britain, since its early beginnings more than one hundred years ago. Every item that it collects has been made by or is connected to British motor manufacturers; 97 known marques were previously extant.

As the BMIHT vehicle and archive collection continued to expand, it was clear that a new home was required. With help from Rover Group, in 1993 the Heritage Motor Centre at Gaydon was opened, enabling many more of the cars in the collection to be put on display and the Archive to be stored in a professional environment.

Now based in an architecturally interesting circular structure, a couple of hours drive from London, close to the former car making crucible of the Midlands and easily accessible from the west, north, or east of the country by direct motorway links, the British Motor Museum is home to the world's largest collection of historic British Cars; it boasts 150 cars on show and nearly 300 cars in its collection which span the classic, vintage and veteran eras, and collections and restorations displays. 120 years of motoring are charted. Because so many of the myriad British independent car makers preserved so much of their works, and because the British Motor Corporation (BMC) and its amalgamation as the colloquially titled British Leyland (BL) had so much to offer, this collection can be rated as a truly world class collection easily ranking in European minds (and beyond) as a true 'conservatoire' across many British marques.

It was the Trust's mission to keep the memory of the British motor industry alive and to tell its story to all, starting from the beginning of the twentieth century to the present day. So a building was designed that not only housed the cars and its extensive motoring archive, but also had educational and conference facilities adding to its usage and viability. Keen to keep the museum current and a leader in its field, in 2006 the Trust was awarded a Heritage Lottery grant of £1.3 million to further enhance the Museums displays and interpretation.

2006 saw the re-development was a new mezzanine floor, which forms a quarter section of the museum and was designed to be a more flexible exhibition space, housing temporary exhibitions – of which many are held.

In November 2014, the Museum was awarded 'Designated Status' – meaning that its collections were of national and international significance. The scheme identifies the pre-eminent collections of national and international importance, based on their quality and significance.

Of particular note is the way that the cars and what they represent have been collated and displayed. Sections are defined on car design, sports cars, motorsport, commercial vehicles. Manufacturers have dedicated stands and rare prototypes – notably those from the great age of BMC and British Leyland design with the cars we nearly saw but that were abandoned at the last hurdle prior to proposed production. Oh, for the Triumph Lynx coupé to have stormed the American market from the basis of its superb TR7 underpinnings! Mini and MG prototypes also provide food for thought on what might have been.

Commercial vehicle and bus enthusiasts will not go unrewarded at this museum. Indeed, it is the cars and archival contents of the British brands and the BMC/BL story that are so well documented, displayed and discussed at this superb museum resource.

Automobilia is well displayed but in a very clean, non-garage setting!

Enthusiasts should know that this museum holds regular events covering learning, research, archival works, and seminars and lectures hosted by experts on subjects as wide-ranging as restoration and writing automotive history.

One of the key features of the British Motor Museum is the Reading Room, which contains an extensive Reference Library including a wide variety of books about motoring and the motor industry. The library is open to museum visitors every day during normal opening hours.

The Reading Room also offers researchers the opportunity to access original material held in the BMIHT Archive store, from the build record of a single vehicle to the entire history of the British Motor Industry. You will need to book an appointment giving at least seven working days' notice, but before you make your arrangements you should establish what material is available in the BMIHT Archive and what you would like to see. This enables the museum team to have the material ready when you arrive so that you can make the most of your visit (fees apply!).

One source is the Discovery website. This resource is part of the National Archives network. Here you can find BMIHT catalogues for the Business Records Collection, the Miles Thomas Papers, the Austin Papers and the Nuffield Papers.

The 65 acres of grounds also allow summer picnics. Car clubs hold regular events in the museum's grounds. The staff at the museum include marque specialists and heritage experts. The Jaguar Daimler Heritage Trust also has a man on hand. Key contacts in the respective departments can be found on the museum's website

The British Motor Museum is 'different' from some of its museum brethren in that it is perhaps a touch more of a niche offering but it is certainly one of great authenticity and, like other leading motor museums, is a place of vital national educational and historical importance. As with a few other museums, it is a true '10 out 10' experience and highly recommended.

BROOKLANDS MUSEUM

Brooklands Road,
Weybridge, Surrey, KT13 0QN, UK.
Telephone: 01932 857381
Opening hours: daily. See website for events and changes.
www.brooklandsmuseum.com

Arguably, this museum is currently the leader of the pack according to many motoring enthusiasts, but it is not just a museum – it is an active altar to our engineering history; a national treasure, but also a living place where mechanical devices live and breathe – working as intended. It may have less static car exhibits than Beaulieu or Haynes, but it does things differently.

Vital British aero-auto-mechanical history is told and crucially re-enacted here. The 'live' events are a super blend of Castrol R, jet fuel, petrol, fumes, noise, classic and vintage atmosphere and wonderful memories. From vintage, veteran and classic to modern classic car clubs, all wheeled and winged history is celebrated and preserved here – as stated, much of it in working order.

Brooklands lives, breathes and smells of all things mechanical. It contains essential British engineering history and also hosts car clubs and marque specific events that are world class in their content and presentation. The famous track and its 'Banking' was designed by Holden, the British motorcycle expert in the early 1900s – and is where the first British motorcycle race was held in 1908.

The 'Racetrack Revival' project has recently seen the original Brooklands racetrack main finishing area uncovered and used for the racing of old cars. I drove a 1914 Chater Lea Special in the opening parade for the revived track and had more fun than can be imagined.

Recent Brooklands Museum Director and CEO Allan Winn, formerly editor of *Flight International*, was the man who, over the much of the last two decades, has driven Brooklands into a new era. He retired from his role in 2018. His successor as chief executive is Tamalie Newberry – former director of the Association of Independent Museums.

An early start is advised if you wish to make the most of a visit to Brooklands. Perhaps on-site glamping should be encouraged to allow a two-day stay over?

The first significant event to celebrate the history of Brooklands was held in 1957 when Vickers-Armstrongs organised a Brooklands Golden Jubilee. One-off events into the 1960s and various on-site preservation works saw the formation of the Brooklands Society with founder members including Lord Montagu of Beaulieu and W. 'Bill' Boddy, the esteemed motoring and motorsport writer.

The 1977 'Wings over Brooklands' exhibition highlighted the uniquely important role that Brooklands had played in the development and history of

international aviation and motoring and following its success, Morag Barton led a move to establish a museum dedicated to the history of Brooklands.

Following British Aerospace's announcement that they were going to sell off the most historic 40 acres of the original Brooklands Motor Racing Circuit, a 99-year lease was entered into in 1984 for 30 of the 40 acres of the site, for the purpose of founding a museum there.

Refurbishment began and the collections grew rapidly. In 1985, the Brooklands Clubhouse and 100 metres of the track were restored by Brooklands benefactors Gallaher Ltd, and Elmbridge Borough Council.

The Vickers Wellington bomber 'R for 'Robert' (Pilot Grp Cpt D. Marwood Elton) was recovered from its wartime Loch Ness ditching, was delivered to Brooklands where it now is exhibited.

In 1987, the Brooklands Museum Trust was launched, with aviation legend Sir Peter Masefield as Chairman and Morag Barton was appointed Museum Director. Many major features of the site were restored or recreated, with the famed 1920s-30s Test Hill re-opened and Members' Bridge reconstructed in 1988, the end of that year seeing the final closure of the British Aerospace factory at Brooklands. Throughout the 1980s and 1990s the collection of Vickers and Hawker aircraft continued to grow and significant vehicles were acquired for long term display.

In April 1989, HRH Prince Michael of Kent became Royal Patron and the Museum was formally opened to the public in 1991.

Over the next few years, new exhibitions and restored buildings were opened and in 1997, the Museum acquired the 1933 ex-John Cobb Napier-Railton with the aid of National Heritage Memorial Fund. Schools took advantage of a structured education programme from the early days of the museum, the first 'Schools Action Day' being held in 1994, and annual motoring and aviation events, including fly-ins, became popular with visitors. Julian Temple made a significant contribution to the evolution of the museum.

July 2001 saw the official opening of the Grand Prix Exhibition in the Jackson Shed and, in 2004, the Sultan of Oman's VC10 airliner, and the Vickers Vanguard Merchantman, which had previously lived on the other side of the river, were relocated to the new Vickers Aircraft Park.

One of the most significant acquisitions in the museum's history was Concorde G-BBDG in 2003 which, after extensive restoration, was opened to the public in 2006. In 2009, the replica Vickers Vimy, which re-enacted the first Trans-Atlantic flight and long distance flights to Australia and South Africa, was donated. The Concorde Simulator was opened in the same year and being taught how to fly Concorde by an ex-Concorde pilot on the Simulator is worth paying for!

In 2012, the 1926 Delage Grand Prix racing car was bequeathed to the Museum. Further significant acquisitions were made in 2013, including important archives from the Bill Boddy estate (including all surviving original BARC minutes books,

scrutineers' notes with racing and track records for Brooklands); the last Vickers VC10 built at Brooklands ZA150, which was flown into Dunsfold and is now maintained in running order there by volunteers. Vickers BAC Chief designer, Sir George Edwards is rightly revered here and his daughter is a regular supporter. In March 2014, the restored Stratosphere Chamber, Control Room and aero-engine display was officially opened by Mary Stopes-Roe, Barnes Wallis's daughter. People like Julian Temple, Max Kingsley-Jones, and others have been key to the realisation of events and themes at Brooklands that make it what it is.

The freehold of the Museum site was gifted to Brooklands Museum Trust by Japan Tobacco International in January 2010 and in August 2011, the new London Bus Museum, which is run by an independent trust, was opened.

Major events continued to attract visitors, including the Centenary Festival in June 2007. The first Dunsfold 'Wings & Wheels' event was staged by Brooklands Museum in 2005 and more recently 'Double Twelve' festivals lead the classic calendar. The Brooklands team have continued to organise the Dunsfold 'satellite' facilities motoring and aviation demonstrations.

Brooklands hosts over 13,000 school children and students on curriculum-based visits every year.

Volunteers have been instrumental in the success of the museum since its earliest times, in restoration, research, fundraising and engaging with visitors. In 2016, the Brooklands Museum volunteers were awarded the Queen's Award for Voluntary Service.

The Brooklands Museum Library contains a large amount of published material relating to all aspects of Brooklands related motoring and aviation. The Technical Archive contains a wealth of information on the aircraft built at Brooklands or by Vickers, BAC, Sopwith, Hawker and BAe. The Photographic Archive includes photographic records of all aspects of the people and cars, motorcycles or bicycles that raced at Brooklands, alongside the aircraft that were built or flew, and the people that worked on them. For further information contact Andrew Lewis via email: andrewlewis@brooklandsmuseum.com.

Brooklands has an atmosphere, a sense of history, and is packed with events, stories and learning. It cannot be anything other than the major jewel in the story of British motoring and aviation.

Key cars on display:

AC Sociable 3-Wheeler 1910
Alta Voiturette 1938
Alvis Clinkard Special 1953
Alvis Front Wheel Drive 1928
Aston Martin 'Razor Blade' 1923
Aston Martin 35hp Tourer 1924

Aston Martin Halford Special 1923-25
Austin 7 Speedy 'Le Mans' 1935
Austin 7 Sports 1937
Austin 7 Ulster 1930
Bentley 4 ½ litre 'Le Mans' 1929
Cooper Climax T51 1960
Cooper T.72 F3 1964
Cuthbert Riley 9hp Special 1929/32
Delage Grand Prix 1927/1926
Duesenberg Single Seater 1927/1931
Elva 100 Formula Junior 1959
Ford 10 Model C 1936
Harper Runabout 1922
Hillman Aero Minx Streamliner 1934
Jordan EJ11 2001
Lagonda M45 Le Mans Replica 1934
Lorraine Dietrich Vieux Charles III 1912
McLaren MP4-21 F1 Show Car (Simulator) 2007
McLaren MP4/6 F1 Show Car 1991
MG Model 'M' Midget 1932
MG PA Sports 1935
Morgan F2 3-wheeler 1937
Morgan JAP 3-wheeler 1929
Morris Eight Saloon 1935
Nanette Brooklands Special 1924
Napier Colonial 1911
Napier-Railton 1933
Olympus Wolf WR7 1979
Peugeot Type 172 Quadrilette 'Grand Sport' 1924
Peugeot Voiture 1900
Railton Terraplane 1934
Ridley Special 1931
Riley Brooklands 1935
Rytecraft 'Scootacar' 1935
Salmson Grand Sport 1925
Siddeley 2-seater tourer 1904
Simtek F1 1994
Singer 9hp Brooklands Racer 1933
Spikins Singer 'The Bantam' 1936
Vauxhall TT 1922
Wolseley Moth 1921

Brooklands is also a mecca for motorcycles, a notable exhibit being the Brough Superior 1000cc 'Works Scrapper'1927. This key display motorcycle was built by Freddie Dixon and the Brough Superior Works to be used in an attempt to take the 'World's Fastest' title.

The motorcycle was a heavily modified SS100 1,000cc machine and was used extensively by Dixon in 1927. He took the record for the first bike with a sidecar to lap Brooklands at over 100 mph and reached 130 mph on a one-way run at Arpajon, France. In 1928, George Brough competed with the bike with speed victories at Pendine Sands and Doncaster among his successes.

In 1929, it was raced by Herbert LeVack, who took the 'World's Fastest' title at Arpajon with an average speed of 129.05 mph over two runs. He also became the first person to ride a motorcycle at more than 200kph (125mph) around the banked circuit at Montlhéry, France.

In 1938, the Brough Works sold the motorcycle to Noel M. Mavrogordato who used it the following year to win the Inter Varsity Sprint at Syston, and a Gold Star for lapping the Brooklands circuit at over 100mph.The machine remained in the Mavrogordato family until 1998, when the present owner acquired it. He has since run it at many revival events, including the Brighton Speed Trials, 'Coupes de Legende' at Montlhery, the Goodwood Festival of Speed and the Festival of 1000 motorcycles.

Motorcycles on display:

ABC Skoota Motor 125cc 1919
ABC Sopwith 398cc 1921
Ariel 500cc Red Hunter 1938
Brough Superior 1000cc 'Works Scrapper' 1927
Brough Superior 1150 with Alpine Grand Sports Sidecar 1933
BSA M23 Empire Star 500cc (replica) 1937
Cotton-Earl JAP 498cc 1928
Douglas 600cc S6 and sidecar 1930
Douglas EW 600cc (reconstruction) 1931
Douglas Works 499cc 1927
Excelsior-Villiers Two Stroke 1938
Francis Barnett 172cc Brooklands Track Special 1927
Grindlay Peerless JAP 500cc 1929
Humber Motorcycle 2 ¾ hp 1904
Kerry-Abingdon 3½ hp 1910
Martinsyde-Newman 680cc 1920
Matchless Silver Arrow 397cc 1930
Norton 'LPD1' 490cc with sidecar 1927
Norton International 350cc 1933
Norton Model 18 500cc 1928

Norton RAC Patrol motorcycle and sidecar 1960
Norton TT Model 18 1927
Norton-Jackson Manx c1950
OK Supreme 350cc JAP 1938
Rex Acme 348cc Blackburne 1926
Rudge 'Brooklands Special' 250cc 1936
Scott 500cc 1925
Sunbeam 493cc 'Light Tourist' 1927
Velocette KSS 348cc Racer 1929
Zenith Bradshaw 3 ½ hp Gradua Drive 1922
Zenith JAP 350cc 1924

Engines on display:

Major 1 1934
de Havilland Gipsy Major 8 1940s/1950s
de Havilland Goblin Mk.3 1942
Junkers Jumo 211 1936
Napier Lion XIA Special 1918/1933 replica
Pratt & Whitney Double Wasp R-2800 1937
Rolls-Royce Avon I – sectioned 1946
Rolls-Royce Avon RA26 1951
Rolls-Royce Conway 540 – sectioned & motorised 1960
Rolls-Royce Dart
Rolls-Royce Dart RD7 1958
Rolls-Royce Dart RDA3 Mk506
Rolls-Royce Derwent Mk 8
Rolls-Royce Kestrel VI (690hp) 1934
Rolls-Royce Merlin 61 1942
Rolls-Royce Merlin XX 1940
Rolls-Royce Nene 1944
Rolls-Royce Turbomeca Adour 1968
Rolls-Royce Tyne Mk 506 1955
Rolls-Royce Welland 1942
Rolls-Royce/Snecma Olympus 593 1966
Rolls-Royce/Snecma Olympus 593 1966
Turbo-Union RB199

Note:
Mercedes-Benz World is also on the Brooklands site and houses over 100 classic
and newer Mercedes-Benz cars and also offers interactive and driving experiences,
facilities including a testing track.

BUBBLE CAR MUSEUM

Clover Farm,
Boston,
PE22 7AW,
Lincolnshire
Telephone: 01285 280037
Opening hours: 1000-1700 Friday, Saturday, Sunday, and Bank Holidays
www.bubblecar museum.co.uk

Bubble car nirvana. Here, at what may be Britain's most unusual motoring museum, can be found over 50 'bubble' or micro cars of a type once fashionable and now being thought about again in a more safety conscious context. Bubble cars were once a vital eco-austerity measure in 1950s Britain. Even Sydney Allard built one (the Clipper), which was not a success.

With prices going beyond £100,000 for a perfect Messerschmitt, it is no surprise that the micro car museum has carved itself a valuable niche as a unique venue where experts are on hand. Even *Wheeler Dealers*, the television show, have tackled bubble cars.

Bond, Isetta, Frisky, Reliant and more all feature in this delightful museum. A display of scooters and motorcycles is also on show here. Bubble car rides are provided on set dates – see website. On-site camping, tea rooms and home-made cake! Perfect for a car club visit too. This museum is bubbly, bizarre and brilliant. But try not to burst your bubble, as plexiglass canopies are very expensive.

BUGATTI TRUST (THE)

Prescott Hill,
Gotherington,
Cheltenham,
Gloucestershire GL52 9
Telephone 0142 677201
Opening hours: Daily except Sundays in Summer. Open on Prescott event weekends.
www.bugatti-trust.co.uk

Medium-sized, utterly authentic and delightfully niche, the Bugatti Trust is one of those rare things, a specialist museum aligned to a single marque and yet which boasts world-class contents, resident experts and a global reach, and respect. This place however is not just for Bugattistes, it is for *anyone* young or old captivated by engineering, design and the Bugatti family's polymath talents.

Housed in a dedicated modern building at Prescott Hill climb, just opposite the separate but close by Bugatti Owners Club headquarters, the Trust is not just a museum but a shrine full of artefacts to the brilliance of the Bugatti family, not just to their cars. With the Prescott Hill Climb on hand, the Trust ensures you can see and hear the amazing sight of Bugattis in action on the track.

Over 1,000 members support the Trust and several of their cars appear here. Education events, exhibitions and outreach/involvement programmes all allow today's youth to become aware of and involved in, engineering and design amid a Bugatti influence. The Trust also supports the Sir Misha Black Awards in honouring the exceptional role of individuals and institution in engineering and design education.

As its founder Hugh Conway Snr said, 'I should be satisfied if as a result of visiting the Trust just one young person takes up a career in mechanical engineering.'

The idea for the Trust began in 1987 when Hugh Conway Snr and Barrie Price were visiting the revered Molsheim museum in Alsace. Price was then Chairman of the Bugatti Owners Club and the idea for a trust and a Bugatti archive collection (rather than a static 'museum') was framed – hence the location alongside and association with the Bugatti Owners Club. Donations, the sales of a Bugatti Type 37, and global fund raising led to the building of the Trust's home and its opening by HRH Prince Phillip Duke of Edinburgh in March 1990.

Today, the curator is Angela Hucke – a dedicated Bugatti expert and driver whose father Uwe Hucke played a large role in Bugatti affairs. The Trust's archive is an international resource with many thousands of factory documents, historic photographs, and books – all of which can be viewed on-line in low-res format via the Trust's website and, can be used for a fee or via membership of the Trust.

Exhibits include numerous Bugatti car types, the Bugatti-designed Bébé Peugeot, aero engines, car engines, furniture, chassis, bodywork, models, and many displays of Bugatti design and motorsport memorabilia. A key achievement was the securing of the Type 59/50 Grand Prix car of J-P. Wimille on long term loan from the Schlumpf Collection /City Museum in 2019. Chassis, and engineering details of Bugattis, including Types 35 and 37 are on show and not roped off – everyone can get up close and learn. Bugatti family design work is also exhibited.

The Trust is about the past, but also about the future and new audiences and new Bugattistes. Small, authentic and truly a 'shrine' to all things Bugatti, the cars are not just static either – they get driven, as they should. This is not an elitist place despite what some may think because of the 'Bugatti' name. Highly recommended, accessible to all and for all ages and even for knowledgeable aficionados. A global resource for Bugattism and engineering education, and of superb quality in all its contexts and contents. Voted Museum of the Year in the 2019 Octane Awards.

The entrance fee is less than the cost of a cup of coffee at a branded outlet and provides a deeper, longer lasting pleasure.

Aerospace at Bristol. The original Bristol Cars grille designed was BMW-inspired, as was its engine.

Above: Inside the smaller museum. Atwell-Wilson Musuem, Calne, provides an eclectic mix. Here is the last of the line Rover SD1 Vitesse twin plenum, surrounded by Saab 99, Toyota Celica. With Vauxhalls, MGs, Triumphs and much more are up close and personal.

Below: Model corner at the smaller museum is always a delight for the enthusiast.

Above: The rare and very interesting Datsun Fairlady and the cars it 'copied' Triumph Spitfire and MGB. This Fairlady at the Atwell-Wilson Museum was purchased new by Standard-Triumph for evaluation and registered to them. All car makers employ such tactics with the competition.

Below: Bicester is brilliant. The Itier Bugatti seen alongside Porsches at the Historit stand on a Bicester open day.

Above: More moments at Bicester – the Overland marque in superb setting. Latterly to become Willys-Overland, this early 1919 Overland Speedster 3.0litre just reeks of authentic automobile history.

Below: Porsche 356 Speedster 'Outlaw' specification seen at Bicester.

Above: Bicester in blue. 993- series Porsche 911 in Riveria Blue at rest. Perfection.

Below: Jaguar's superb XJ13 seen at the British Motor Museum. Mid-engined magic. (Photo: BMM)

Above: Forgotten Jaguar racer – the XJ coupé racer preserved for posterity. (Photo: BMM)

Right: The curious incident of the Austin Metropolitan. Not as nice as the Nash Healey. Seen at the British Motor Museum. (Photo: BMM)

Above: The rare, cut-away Allegro in store with other BMC/BLgems. (Photo: BMM)

Below: The Bugatti Trust – a superb smaller museum yet one with a global influence and a stunning collection.

Right: The Peugeot 'Baby' (Bugatti-designed) emerges from the main hall at the Bugatti Trust at Prescott. Old cars must be driven.

Below: Engineering details of the Bugatti T35 series chassis seen at the Bugatti Trust.

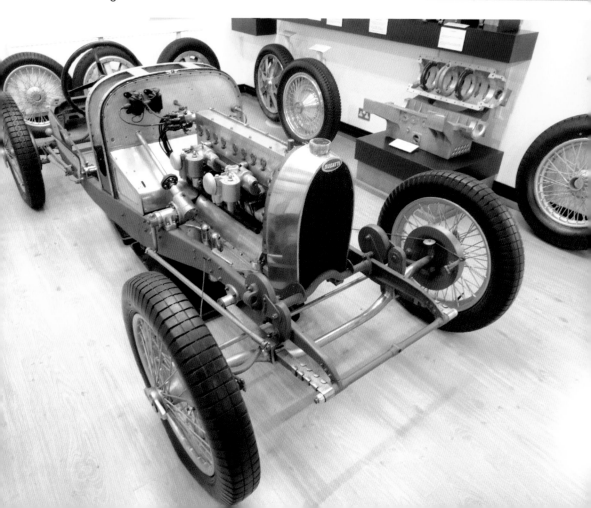

The Bugatti Trust and the Bugatti Owners Club managed to secure loan of the J-P Wimille T59/50B machine from its French home at Citie de l'Automobile (including the former Schlumph collection).

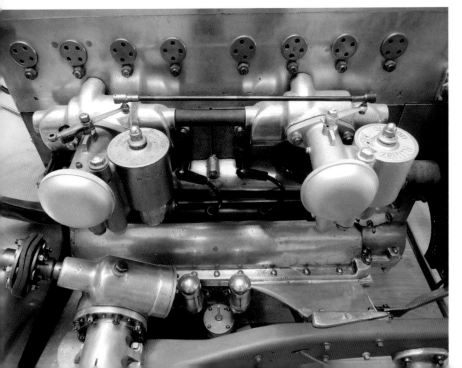

Engines exposed – Bugatti Type 35 straight-eight on display at Prescott.

Brooklands action – opening up the re-exposed original start straight.

Brooklands atmosphere – up close and personal and the real thing.

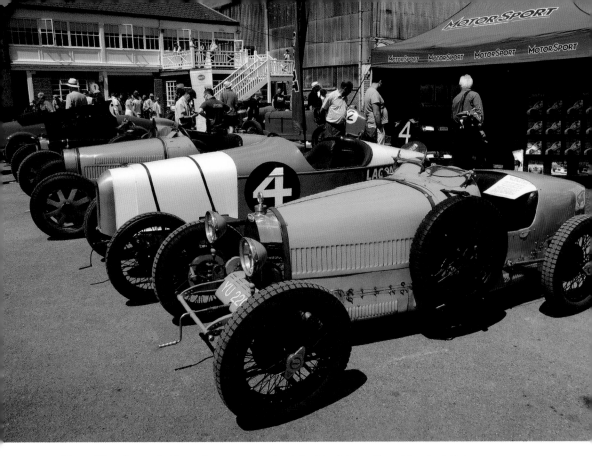

Above: Blue Bugatti, *Motor Sport* tent and original buildings. Brooklands delight.

Below: Commercials can be delightful. This Citroën van is part of the Yapp Brothers French collection that includes a Traction Avant.

Volunteers make many museums possible. The late Christopher Orlebar, VC10 and Concorde pilot, MGB GT owner, was a volunteer at Brooklands and friend of many.

An Italian diorama. Seen at Goodwood, it's nostalgia on steroids.

There is a big 'woodies' subculture and this Bentley 'half-timbered' car was superb.

Above: The joy of nameplates. As applied to a pre-1922 GN with a French body.

Opposite: Autojumble, this time at Loheac Museum in France.

Above: Americarna, Ford Galaxie 500 captured at Prescott on American Day.

Below: BMC's Pininfarina-designed Austin/Morris design was a huge success. Displayed in the corner of a smaller museum.

Above and below: Inside the excellent Lakeland Museum where access to cars is up close and vital. (Photos: Lakeland Museum)

Lakeland tributes the Campbell exploits in brilliant blue hue.

Opposite: First World War display at the Lakeland Museum.

CAISTER CASTLE MUSEUM

Castle Lane, Caister-on-Sea,
Great Yarmouth,
Norfolk, NR30 5SN.
Opening hours: 1000-1630 weekdays. Closed Sundays. Open May to September
www.caistercastele.com

Stuck way out east on the Anglian peninsula, Caister is a long-established museum that we can truly say is off the beaten track. Set amid a castle ruin, Caister offers vintage, classic, and modern classic offerings – right up to the Ford Fiesta. An 1893 Panhard et Lavassor is in residence, as is a Jim Clark Lotus, examples of Bentley, Bugatti and motorcycles across several eras. Assorted mechanicals in the form of bicycles, horse-drawn devices, pedal cars and agricultural implements are also on show.

Although a smaller offering in the national motor museum experience, Caister is however a genuine and long-established museum and well worth a visit.

CANVEY ISLAND TRANSPORT MUSEUM (CASTLE POINT)

105 Point Road,
Canvey Island,
Essex, SS8 7TD. UK.
Telephone: 01268 684272
Email: Info@castlepointtransportmuseum.co.uk
www.castlepointtransportmuseum.co.uk

Canvey Island is off the beaten track, but for the true enthusiast, this museum provides the essential ingredients. Canvey Island Transport Museum (also known as Castle Point Museum) celebrated its 40th Anniversary in 2019. The building that houses the Museum was built in 1934 for the Canvey & District Motor Transport Co. Ltd. and served a series of transport companies before passing to the Eastern National Omnibus Co. Ltd, which used it until 1978.

The Castle Point Transport Museum Society then acquired the leasehold of the depot, later purchasing the freehold, and has since assembled a collection of

30-plus preserved commercial vehicles, these now forming the museum's main display. Visitors can see classic examples from marques such as AEC, Bedford, Bristol, Guy, and Leyland, plus legendary coachbuilders like Eastern Coach Works, Duple, Harrington and Massey Brothers.

While many vehicles are fully restored, others are being rebuilt and undergoing maintenance by their owners or groups of members in the open-to-access workshops.

Visitors can also see traditional techniques like wood-frame construction and aluminium panel beating. In addition, the Museum has its own impressive model railway layout, plus there is a wide variety of transport artefacts on display. The Museum shop sells die-cast models, souvenirs and other transport related merchandise.

JIM CLARK MUSEUM

44 Newton Street,
Duns, TD11 3AU.
Scotland.
New museum run by Jim Clark Trust.
www.jimclarktrust.com

Opened as early as 1966, this used to be known as the Jim Clark Room and was his home town's tribute to a true racer. Sadly this great talent and person that was Jim Clark died tragically early, yet today, decades later, the 'room' has metamorphosed into a new home as a small museum containing trophies, memorabilia, and poignant memories of what was, and what should have been. Re-opened in 2019 as a more fitting tribute, this will surely become a small, but key stop on the motorsport museum landscape.

CLOVERLANDS MODEL CAR MUSEUM

Montgomery Institute, Arthur Street,
Montgomery, Powys,
SY15 6RA.UK.
Telephone: 01686 668004
www.cloverlandsmuseum.org.uk

Small, but vital if your like model cars and are in the area.

CRAVEN MOTORCYCLE MUSEUM

Brockfield Villa, Stockton-on-Forest,
York, YO32 9UW.
Telephone:0190 4400493
www.cravencollection.co.uk

Here lies a personal and engaging collection of classic motorcycles with nearly 300 classic machines on show – spanning from 1920s to recent years, plus what the museum calls a 'mountain of motoring memorabilia'.

Housed in an old farm building and opened in 1994, Mr I.R. Craven bought and restored motorcycles, which was how the museum began its life.

The British bike section has over 200 bikes spanning from 1918 to 1987. The Japanese section has about 40 bikes and there is also a sidecar section. Of note, special displays cover military, police, trials, and four-wheeled motorcycles and their variants. The museum also owns two dozen 1950s-1960 classic cars and commercial vehicles. This museum is typical of the effort, enthusiasm and personal commitment evident amid the layers or sub-cultures of British museums. For the motorcyclist, from vintagent to modern classicist, this museum may be smaller, less glamorous, yet is well worth time spent.

CRICH TRAMWAY MUSEUM

Crich,
Matlock, Derbyshire, DE4 5DP.UK.
Telephone: 01773 854 321
Opening hours: 1000-1700 daily in high season
www.tramway.co.uk

Is this the best tram museum in the world? Possibly, and it is less petroliana and more electroliana for certain.

Operated by the Tramway Museum Society as a registered charity as a 'national' tram museum, this is certainly a highly recommended offering that delivers on its promises. Funded by the Wolfson Foundation and Derbyshire Economic Forum Partnership, the museum has entered the 'new age' of the museum without losing its soul or the point of its existence – the vehicles themselves.

After a 2010 'Century of Trams' revamp, the exhibitions are even better, and the sheer diversity of trams on show really is something to indulge in, not least from a design and styling standpoint across 150 years. 2019 has seen further expansion to the exhibits and learning on offer via a focus on the little-known

yet pioneering nineteenth century inventor Michael Holroyd-Smith who created Britain's first electric tramway in Blackpool in 1885. Note the 'helicopters and boomerangs' heading to his display if you visit. He was also involved in early electric railways and is an 'invisible' hero of industrial design and engineering – including automotive and aeronautical applications.

With a working one mile tramway offering plenty of rides on the trams, several halls of exhibitions, a superb cafe and other family-friendly, non-tram related but on-site attractions as part of a 'village', this is a place that meets the needs of dedicated enthusiasts and also of families.

From 1860 to the 1950s, all tram life is here and many are superbly restored without losing much originality. An excellent archives and records service is available.

Trams may be niche, but that should not stop us enjoying their rich engineering and design heritage. The museum's web site is also informative and easy to navigate.

Packed with tram and tramways exhibits and education, this museum is another 'hidden gem' deserving of support and recognition. It is a true star amid the blend of the old and the new in museum culture and management.

COTSWOLD MOTORING MUSEUM AND TOY COLLECTION

The Old Mill,
Bourton-on-the-Water,
Gloucestershire, GL54 2BY. UK.
Opening times: 1000-1700 seven days a week from February-December
Telephone; 01451 821 255
museum@cotswildmotormseum.co.uk

Parked next to the River Windrush in the Cotswolds, this is a motoring museum with over 50 cars on display that is also populated with toys as museum pieces amid a selection of classic or vintage caravans, motorcycles and delights such as enamel signs and what the museum call 'motoring curiosities'. Intriguingly, the museum is owned and operated by a trading arm of the Civil Service Motoring Association (CSMA); a discount on the entry fee is worth remembering for CSMA members – of which there are many in Great Britain. CSMA has existed since as early as the 1920s – a fact often regretfully overlooked by those who take a certain view of it.

A replica period garage and walls hung with much motoring ephemera add to the atmosphere of this small but interesting museum. The 'toy collection' description hardly does justice to the gathering of toy cars. The museum is also

home to 'Brum', the TV car character. A display of 1960 and 1970s British cars in the Paradise gallery evokes a certain period of 'my dad had one of those' nostalgia.

At over 7, 500sq.ft in area, with seven galleries, this is a smaller museum yet one that is a gem of an affair and in no way a 'lesser' museum. Easily visitable and ideal for a day out, it also offers families and children a stepping stone into tasting our motoring past.

COVENTRY TRANSPORT MUSEUM

Coventry Transport Museum,
Millennium Place,
Hales Street,
Coventry,
CV1 1JD.UK.
Telephone: 024 7623 4270
Opening times: 1000-1700.
www.transport-museum.com

Housing the world's largest collection of British road transport vehicles, the Coventry Transport Museum offers something slightly out of the ordinary. As well as a collection of bikes, the museum also houses Thrust SSC and Thrust 2 and loads of cool two, three, four and many more-wheeled vehicles.

The long-established museum tells the fascinating story of Coventry and its people through the rise and fall of its biggest industry – car, motorcycle and bicycle manufacturing. Originally opened in 1980 at its Cook Street location, the museum contains a strong collection of cars, motorcycles, and of note Midlands-built bicycles dating from the dawn of cycle manufacture as velocipedes. A motorised bicycle known as the Edward Butler of 1887 pre-dates the 1890s origins of the true motorcycle.

Now fully re-open after a £9.5m redevelopment programme, this huge museum offers a detailed day out in an iconic city-centre building and is completely free.

DAVID BROWN TRACTOR MUSEUM

PO Box 990,
Holmfirth,
West Yorkshire, HD9 1YH, UK.
See website for selected opening dates and times.
www.dbtc.co.uk

Run by the David Brown Tractor Club volunteers, with approximately 20 tractors in the museum, many are historic and of significance in DB history. One for tractor buffs and possibly Aston Martin enthusiasts of agricultural vein.

DAVID COULTHARD MUSEUM

Ashland, Twynholm,
Dumfries and Galloway,
DG6 4NP, Scotland.
Telephone: 01557 860 608
www.coulthardmuseum.com

You will need to be a Formula One fan and perhaps also a David Coulthard fan to want or need to specifically travel to visit this collection – but it is also well worth a visit for those motoring fans who journey to it or happen to be passing through the forgotten and wonderful corner of south west Scotland. Carry on to the bookshops of Wigtown to enjoy Scotland's second hand bookshop capital. The Solway Firth and Whithorn, should not be missed either. Now called Dumfries and Galloway, this was once the land of standing stones, forests and coastline. Definitely worth a visit.

The David Coulthard Museum displays the world's most complete collection of race cars and memorabilia collected by any Formula 1 driver, past or present.

The collection was originally started by David's parents, Duncan and Joyce, who bought him his first go-kart for Christmas when he was 12 years old. This kart, together with examples of cars from all formulas which David has participated in, are on display. During David's fourteen years in formula one, he won 13 Grand Prix, had 62 podium finishes, achieved 12 pole positions and 18 fastest laps. David is now of course world famous as a motorsport commentator and broadcaster and retains the respect of many fans and people in motorsport. This small museum is a charming tribute to a much admired figure.

DAVID SILVER HONDA COLLECTION

Leiston, Suffolk. UK.
Open Monday-Friday 0900-1700. 0900-1600 Saturday.
www.davidsilvercollections.co.uk

A more recently established emporium, the David Silver collection is one of the UK's least known motorcycling gems. Opened in 2016 and located in East Anglia

at Leiston. This museum is the work of renowned classic Honda parts specialist David Silver and is devoted to classic Hondas. 150 different models, ranging from a Super Cub to CBR900RR FireBlade, are on display. Bikers will love it.

DESIGN MUSEUM LONDON

224-238 Kensington High Street,
London, W8 6AG, UK.
Opening hours: 1000-1800. Check for changes
wwwdesignmuseum.org

London it may be, but always worth keeping up to date with the Design Museum has kept in tune with automotive and industrial design and cars. The museum and a certain not unconnected Mr S.Bayley, have always celebrated classic cars and fine design. Perhaps the Design Museum might be a touch too esoteric for your average 'oily rag' flat-cap classic car enthusiast, but there is no harm in an open mind. At one time, it hosted a Saab 900 Turbo Classic as a work of art. Even Lutz 'Luigi' Colani the king of streamlining has had a retrospective show at the Design Museum. Ferraris have featured in more recent years, with an emphasis on the art of coachbuilding and design couture.

DOVER TRANSPORT MUSEUM

Willingdon Road,Whitfield,
Dover, Kent,
CT16 2JX.UK.
Telephone: 01304 822409
Note variable opening times on seasonal basis. March-October open Wednesday, Saturday and Sunday 1030- 1700.
www.dovertransportmuseum.org.uk

This museum is home to many forms of vintage transport and also features vintage shop fronts. Set in two acres, over 100 vehicles are on display and the place is packed with memorabilia and interesting artefacts. With a large visitor-operated model railway and a taxi & bus hunt for children, family visits are well catered for.

Main exhibits include, cars, commercials, trams, motorcycles, engines, steam engines, and model cars. An interesting and rare display of motorcycles manufactured by the Norman company, are featured.

Well worth a visit; filled with interesting exhibits, there is enough here for the true enthusiast as well as the family visitor.

DUNDEE TRANSPORT MUSEUM

Unit 10, Market Mews,
Market Street,
Dundee, DD1 3LA,
Scotland.
Telephone 01382 455196
Opening hours: Winter; Wednesday, Saturday, Sunday 1030 to 1530: Summer;
Monday and Wednesday.
www.dmoft.co.uk

Opened in 2014 and temporarily housed in the centre of Dundee while fund
raising to restore the old Maryfield tram and bus sheds as a permanent home, this
is another, smaller, charity status affair that is a recently accredited museum and
one of real quality and enjoyment. It has great collection of interest to anyone,
not just locals – even if the focus is local transport. A series of interesting annual
events and gatherings ensure plenty of profile and visitors. These special day events
include a respected, bi-annual steam event, a 'Truck Extravaganza', gatherings of
buses and coaches. The museum hosts an annual Dundee Motor Show.

Exhibits range from veteran, vintage and post-1939 classic cars and vehicles,
up to modern classics. Trams, buses, lorries, steam engines, bicycles, motorcycles,
marine, artefacts and memorabilia populate the displays – which are open access
and touchable. The diverse list of displays includes modern classics such as the
Audi Quatrro; Austin A35; Police Hillman Imp; Jaguar XK150; Mk10, Bedford
and Leyland commercials; the Enfield electric car; Chitty Chitty Bang Bang and
plethora of commercials, motorcycles, a good collection of buses, as well as
marine exhibits and miniature and model railways. A recent display car was the
Practical Classics magazine Standard Nine which was saved from scrapping and
wonderfully fettled in Dundee.

This is a super, smaller museum devoid of 'bling' or digital displays (no bad
thing), but utterly authentic and accessible. Awaiting a more historic building for
its home, there is content here for the serious enthusiast as well as the family visit.
Not to be missed if you are in the region. Cake correctly served in the cafe!

DUNSFOLD COLLECTION (THE)

Whispers, Guildford Road,
Cranleigh, GU6 8PR, UK.
Telephone: 011753 880594
www.dunsfoldcollection.co.uk

A collection of Land-Rovers within a registered charity/trust and stemming from a private collection started in 1968 by Brian Bashall, has created an important record and resource of the vital Land-Rover – truly an 'icon' as the word is intended. Over 130 significant Land-Rovers across all its chassis concepts and contexts are present. Land-Rover archive material and artefacts also within the collection.

Note, the collection is now only open for viewing via dedicated events and special days such as the 'open weekend'. See website for details.

FERGUSON FAMILY MUSEUM

Copse Lane, Freshwater,
Isle of Wight, PO40 9TL, UK.
Telephone: 01983 752347
See website for opening times
www.ferguson-museum.co.uk

The Ferguson Family Museum celebrates the life of tractor pioneer Harry Ferguson. It depicts his life and interest in aviation, Grand-Prix racing and, of course, tractors and agricultural implements which made him famous. He was world famous for his 'Little Grey Fergie' but many people are unaware of his engineering achievements in other fields. The museum contains numerous unique exhibits and photos and Museum Curator Peter Warr, who worked for Harry Ferguson for many years, provides a wealth of information and anecdotes that bring the museum alive. This small personal museum is a must for all enthusiasts and is open by appointment at a charge of £6.50 (discounts available for groups). Location; the museum is located alongside the working farmyard of Harry Ferguson Farms Ltd at Kings Manor, Freshwater, Isle of Wight. The surrounding countryside is some of the finest in the country and the museum is only a short walk for yachtsman visiting Yarmouth Harbour as well as being close to the well-known Red Lion Pub.

FILCHING MANOR MOTOR MUSEUM (FOULKES HALBARD COLLECTION)

Filching Manor, Jevington Road,
Wannock, Polegate,

East Sussex, BN26 5QA.
Telephone: 01323 487124.
Check for opening hours.
foulkeshalbard@aol.com
campbellcircuit.co.uk

Readers of a certain age will be more familiar with this wonderful family-established 'emporium' than others. Those who have read *The Automobile* since its earlier days will have followed (the late) Paul Foulkes Halbard in his dealings as a collector and purveyor of classic, vintage and veteran cars (originally at Smugglers Lane, Crowborough) and the establishment of a Filching Manor collection as a museum amid a stunning setting nestling under the Sussex Downs, an ancient house (circa 1450) and a family name and history that can be traced back across the centuries.

Paul helped rescue the unique 1940s Don Juan Ovidio Alesso *monposto* Special with flat-12 configuration project which is housed at the museum. Paul was involved in the Bexhill motoring pageant as well as other local initiatives. Well known in his field, often in the motoring media, and a dedicated projects man, Paul died in his sixties and left a large gap in his niched world. Now curated by Paul's son Karl and mother Greta, this rare offering of an interesting and varied collection of cars and memorabilia in a large barn, includes an 1890 Bergmann Orient 'Express' Type Six (one of two left in working order), a 1907 Corbin racer, several Bugattis, Fangio's own racing car, and a 1904 chain-driven Mercedes. Of note, Filching's cars are in working order and often exercised.

Also sitting within the Filching environs is the Campbell Circuit karting site. The collection has a Campbell family-focus and contains cars, boats and memorabilia associated with the Campbell father and son duo and descendant, Gina. Of note, the Saunders-Roe-built, Rolls-Royce-powered K3 of Sir Malcolm Campbell of 1938 is evident and in restored, fine fettle. However, of motoring interest, a veritable platter of veteran-class early cars, desirable Bugattis, Edwardian, and 1920s-1930s racing esoterica have passed through Filching's gates and some remain exhibited here. Filching's also played a role in the development of the Bexhill Motoring Festival.

The ceilings and walls hang with auto-mechanical-aero-marine artefacts, memorabilia, parts, models, and signs.

Foulkes Halbard at Filching is not habitually open on a daily basis and appointments are advised, although it often says it is 'open' on Saturdays. Car clubs are welcome, and regular planned marque visits occur. Club secretaries are advised to telephone well in advance.

Filching is clearly one for the true enthusiast, old cars and historical 'stuff' being the focused theme. In my opinion Filching is a 100 per cent authentic, 'car-people' place.

Key exhibits include:

1890 Bergmann Orient 'Express' Type Six
1895 rotary action engine
1907 Corbin
1916 Marmon
1926 Amilcar
Bugatti T13, T35, T48,
1904 Mercedes
1933 Vale Special and other motorcycles,
1940s Alesso Special
Campbell K3 power boat
Gina Campbell boats and memorabilia
Assorted motoring and motorcycling memorabilia (note DKW streamliner body)
Leo Villa's (Campbell's mechanic) memorabilia

Note associated karting track – which is family friendly.

FORD HERITAGE CENTRE

Dagenham,
Essex, RM9 6PG.

Surprisingly small and of 'warehouse' style, this is where Ford keeps its collection of British-built, or British designed cars. Not open to the public, nor open on a daily basis, it is accessible via special 'heritage open days' and is easier to attend via appointment for your car club. If you are Ford fan, this is blue-oval heaven, just do not expect modern museum experience. It's a workshop and store and it's about cars.

GLENLUCE MOTOR MUSEUM

Glenluce,
Nr Newton Stewart,
(Wigtownshire)
Dumfries and Galloway,
DG8 0NY,

Scotland.
Telephone: 01581 300534
Check for opening hours.

A small collection of vintage and classic cars, motorcycles, memorabilia and a vintage-style garage. Located in 'forgotten' corner of Scotland close to Wigtown – Scottish capital of second-hand book shops – the Glenluce Museum has been going for years yet it is very hard to get information upon. Reportedly, it is authentic, small and good for a look around and a dig about. Best to ring ahead – as in days of old on something called a land line.

GLOUCESTER MUSEUM & ARCHIVES/ GLOUCESTER HERITAGE

Brunswick Road,
Gloucester.
GL1 1HP. UK.
Opening hours: 1000-1700 except Sunday

A vital resource for those interested in Gloucester's very strong road, rail and, notably, maritime and aviation history. Also see Gloucester Transport Museum and the Museum of the Jet Age.

In case you don't know, Cotton motorcycles were Gloucester-made. Gloucester aircraft could not really have come from anywhere else. The car, motorcycle, and aviation industries all have significant places in Gloucester's history.

A superb web-resource is Alan Drewett's 'Gloucestershire Transport History'.

The annual 'Gloucestershire Steam fair and Extravaganza' at South Cerney is one of the best classic vehicle events in the country and many people stay over for the three days.

GRAMPIAN TRANSPORT MUSEUM

Alford,
Aberdeenshire,
AB33 8AE, Scotland.
Telephone: 01975 562292
See website for opening hours
Website: www.gtm.org.uk

The museum is a living museum, according to its website. Many exhibits are climb aboard, hands on and even ride-on. The exhibits are updated every year during the closed season, providing a wide range of new things to see each year.

Throughout the year, the museum has an extensive outdoor events programme, with such events taking place as Alford SpeedFest, Grampian Motorcycle Convention, Family Fun Days, and How Many Left?

Grampian Transport Museum continues to build on strengths that won it the title of 'Visitor Attraction of the Year' at the 2014 Aberdeen City & Shire Tourism Awards, and is home to the Visitor Information Centre for the area. Another small gem of a museum, one devoid of profile and bling, but utterly authentic. Well worth a visit, especially on an event day. Bring a coat, it can be cold here even in June!

HAYNES INTERNATIONAL MOTOR MUSEUM

Sparkford,
Yeovil,
Somerset,
BA22 7LH.UK
Opening hours: Monday-Saturday 0930-1730 except major national holidays
www.haynesmotormuseum.com

Nestled in wonderful Somerset – so often by-passed by westward-bound tourists intent on speeding along the scenic A303 dual carriageway – there lies a collection of low buildings (recently revamped) that contain some of the world's most important old cars and motorsport legends. The Haynes collection represents motoring from the 1800s to the present day. Here lies John Haynes' emporium and achievement – a museum of truly international standing and one that contains essential examples of British and overseas car manufacturing history. One man's vision achieved much. He earned the money to pay for it himself – through his big idea – the Haynes manual. Sadly, John died recently.

The Haynes International Motor Museum at Sparkford is home to more than 400 cars and motorbikes, and is Britain's biggest motor museum (by numbers). The museum was originally opened in 1985 by John Haynes, founder of Haynes Publishing Group, who hoped it would run alongside his workshop manual business. The Museum was opened by the then Land Speed Record holder Richard Noble OBE. Since its opening, the collection's international theme has expanded as vehicles from around the globe were acquired in increasing numbers, from 'just' 29 at origin to nearly 400 in 30 years.

Preservation-by-operation is key to the cars of the collection; cars and motorcycles are made to be used – driven, so at Haynes, special visitor events are run for the museum's range of cars and motorcycles. Car Clubs also visit. Robin Morley's excellent annual UK 'Swedish Day' Saab and Volvo festival was based at Haynes until the recent expansion enforced a move.

Inside the Haynes museum, an array of themes and respective displays capture the many aspects of our motoring and motorsport heritage. The American Collection is significant and includes all the muscle cars from the early twentieth century onwards. American classic car fans with interests from the 1930s to the 1970s will not be disappointed. The 'Vroom Room' – part of the recent revamp – features a number of supercars, including a Lamborghini Countach.

The Red Room is well known as dedicated a hall of red-hued racers, including cars driven by Michael Schumacher and Sir Stirling Moss, while new exhibits include Mark Webber's RB6 Red Bull Formula One car – which was blue!

British post-war-classics, 1960s-1970s classics, modern classics, motorcycles, memorabilia and of course, Haynes manuals, all populate this superb museum which requires a day to fully explore. Most cars are accessible and you can get up close, although some gems are roped off. Pre-booked appointments with the archive/curatorial office will help the researcher make the most of the Haynes memorabilia and automobilia collections.

Popular and fascinating, the Haynes as it is colloquially known, comes highly recommended.

Haynes key exhibits include:

AC Frua Convertible 1972
AC Ace-Bristol 1956
AJS R12 1930
AJS Model 39 Silver Streak 1939
AJS 500 Twin 1955
Albion LCA44 Van 1934
Alfa Romeo Spider Veloce 1968
Alfa Romeo 164 1994
Alfa Romeo 6C 1750 Gran
   Tourismo 1929
Alfa Romeo Giulia Sprint 1967
Alfa Romeo Spider 1996
Alfa Romeo Spider 2600 1963
Allard K1 Two Seater Sports 1947
Alvis Speed 20/25 1934
Alvis TD21 Series 1 Drop Head
   Coupé 1960

Ambassador Ambassador 1960
Armstrong Siddeley Star Sapphire
   1959
Aston Martin DB2 1952
Aston Martin DBS GT 1967
Aston Martin Lagonda 1982
Auburn 852 Speedster 1936
Austin 16/6 Carlton 1934
Austin A35 Saloon 1957
Austin A40 Somerset 1954
Austin A90 Atlantic 1952
Austin Mini cutaway 1960
Austin Mini-Moke 1964
Austin 10 Saloon 1934
Austin Healey 100/6 1956
Austin Healey Sprite Mk1 1959
Austin Nash Metropolitan 1960

Bajaj Auto Rickshaw 1994

Bentley Arnage Red Label 2000

Bentley 4.5 DHC 1930

Bentley Continental GTC 2007

Bentley S3 Saloon 1965

Bentley S1 Saloon 1957

Bentley Continental 1987

Bentley S2 Continental 1960

Benz Patent Motorwagon (replica) 1885

BL Mini 9X prototype 1978

BMC Austin Mini 1965

BMW C1 200 2001

BMW 2002 1973

BMW 3 Litre CSi Coupe 1973

Bricklin SV1 1975

Bricklin SV-1 1975

Bristol 403 1953

British Leyland Mini Prototype 1978

Brough Superior SS80 and sidecar 1937

BSA Bantam D1 125 Racer 1951

BSA AA Motorcycle Combination 1960

BSA Bantam D14/4 1968

BSA 557cc 'Flat Tank' 1914

BSA A7 Gold Star 1949

BSA 493cc ohv Speedway Bike 1929

Buick Series 40 2 Door Coupe 1940

Cadillac Fleetwood Sedan 1949

Cadillac Model 452 V16 1931

Cadillac Sedan de Ville 1959

Cadillac de Ville 1965

Cadillac Eldorado 1974

Caterham Super 7 1990

Chevrolet Corvette Convertible 2006

Chevrolet Corvette Stingray 1963

Chevrolet Corvette Stingray 1969

Chevrolet El Camino SS 396 Pick-Up 1970

Chevrolet Fleetline Aero Sedan 1947

Chevrolet Custom Pick-up Truck 1941

Chevrolet Fleetline Deluxe 1949

Chevrolet Camaro SS 1967

Chevrolet Impala SS 1964

Chevrolet Camaro Z28 1978

Chevrolet Bel Air 1955

Chevrolet Corvette 1960

Chevrolet Corvette 1985

Chevrolet Corvette C5 2001

Citroen DS 19A 1967

Citroen 11 CV 1955

Citroen SM Coupe 1973

Citroen 2CV 1958

Citroen 5CV Cloverleaf 1922

Citroen Saxo 2001

Clement Voiturette 1899

Cord Beverley 1935

Crocker Speedway Bike 1934

Cyclemaster Piatti 1956

CZ 175 Sports 1972

DAF 44 Saloon 1971

Daimler Wagonette 1897

Daimler SP 250 Dart 1963

Daimler Detachable top limo 1905

Daimler Conquest 1954

Daimler Double Six Coupe 1975

Daimler Ferret Scout Car 1966

Daimler Light Thirty Phaeton 1919

Darracq Type L 1903

Datsun 240Z Coupe 1972

De Tomaso Pantera 1972

Delahaye 135 Course 1936

Delahaye 135M Cabriolet 1939

Delorean DMC-12 1981

DKW W2000 1977

Dodge Viper RT10 1995
Dodge Charger 1969
Douglas DT5 Dirt Track 1928
Duesenberg Model J 1931
Elva Courier 1959
Empire Model 31 1913
Excelsior Warrior 1936
Excelsior JAP MK1 1939
Excelsior JAP MK2 1948
Facel Vega HK500 1958
Ferrari 250 GT Cabriolet 1960
Ferrari 456 GTA 1997
Ferrari 308 GTSi 1981
Ferrari California 2009
Ferrari Modena 360 Spider 2000
Ferrari 400i 1982
Ferrari F310 F1 1996
Ferrari F360 GT 2002
FIAT 600D 1965
FIAT 500 Topolino 1954
Ford Edsel Station Wagon 1959
Ford Model T Hot Rod 1979
Ford Escort Mexico 1971
Ford Model B 1934
Ford 105E Anglia 1966
Ford Fairlane 500 Skyliner
   Retractable 1958
Ford Anglia 1955
Ford Mustang convertible 1966
Ford V8 Model 78 Deluxe
   'Woody' 1937
Ford GT40 MkII (replica) 1966
Ford Capri 2 Litre GTL 1973
Ford Sierra RS 500 Duckhams
   1987
Ford Model T 1915
Ford Consul 1961
Ford Thunderbird convertible
   1959
Ford Cortina Mk1 1965
Ford V8 Pilot 1950

Ford 103E Popular 1959
Ford Sierra Cosworth 1987
Ford GT40 Dax replica 1994
Ford Zephyr Custom 1961
Ford Mustang GT Conv 2005
Ford LTD Country Squire 1979
Ford Convair 1960
Francis Barnett Model 3 1923
Gaz M13 Chaika 1959
Gilbern Invader Estate 1971
Ginetta G15 1970
Godden GR500 1980
Gordon Keeble GK1 1965
Hagon Cole JAP Speedway Bike
   1960
Harley Davidson Fat Boy 1992
Harley Davidson Duoglide 1958
Harper Scootermobile 1954
   British Scooters 1919 - 1970
Haynes Chassis (Poss Light 12)
Haynes Light 12 1917
Haynes Special
Healey Silverstone 1950
Heinkel Kabine 1956
Hillman Minx Mk 8 1954
Hillman Imp Californian 1967
Hindustan Ambassador 1992
Honda N600 AT 1971
Honda CB72 Dream 1965
Honda Combi 1975
Horstmann Horstmann 1915
Humber Hawk 1967
Humber Sceptre 1971
Humber Super Snipe cutaway 1946
Indian Dirt Track 1927
ISO Fidia 1971
Jaguar E Type V12 S3 1973
Jaguar XKSS replica 1957
Jaguar Mk VIII Saloon 1957
Jaguar XKR Conv 1998
Jaguar 3.5 Litre Saloon 1949

Jaguar 420 G 1969

Jaguar E Type Series 1, 4.2 Fixed Head Coupe 1965

Jaguar Mk2 2.4 Litre Saloon 1968

Jaguar XK120 1951

Jaguar XJ220 1995

Jaguar XK150 Drop Head Coupe 1959

Jaguar D-Type Longnose (replica) 1988

James Autocycle 1939

Jawa 2 Valve 1968

Jawa Briggo 1975

Jawa ERM 1975

Jawa Model 897 1986

Jeep CJ7 Renegade 1984

Jensen Interceptor Mk3 1973

Jensen CV8 Mk1 1963

Jensen Healey Jensen Healey 1975

Jordan Playboy Roadster 1928

Jowett Javelin 1952

Kermond JAP 1950

Kougar Kougar 1968

Lagonda LG45 DHC 1937

Lamborghini LP400S Countach 1981

Lambretta LI Slimline 1963

Lanchester 30 HP Sports Tourer 1929

Lancia Flavia 1966

Land Rover Series 2 Pick-up 1958

Langton JAP 1948

Lincoln Continental Town Car 1979

Lincoln Zephyr 4 Door Sedan 1938

Lola Cosworth T370/HU3 F1 1975

Lotus Elan S3 1967

Lotus Elise 1996

Lotus Elite 503 1977

Lotus Europa S2 Type 54 1971

Lotus Elite Sorts Coupe 1959

Lotus Esprit Turbo 1981

March 86C 1986

Marcos 3 Litre 1969

Marendaz 13/70 Special 1934

Maserati Merak SS 1982

Matchless G80 1949

Mazda Eunos 1990

Mercedes 190SL 1961

Mercedes 280SL 1970

Mercedes 450 SEL 6.9 1979

Mercedes 450 SLC 1974

Messerschmitt KR200 1961

Metrocab Taxi 1997

MG MGA 1600 Roadster 1960

MG MGC GT 1969

MG MGF 1995

MG M Type Midget 1930

MG Midget 1968

MG TC 1947

MG TF 1955

MG MGB Roadster 1967

MG Magnette ZA 1955

MG TA 1938

Moon Model 642 Touring Car 1920

Morgan Super Sport 1933

Morgan Plus 8 1980

Morris Minor Tourer (Convertible) 1955

Morris Mini Cooper 1965

Morris 10/4 Tourer 1933

Morris Minor Van 1935

Morris Cowley 'Bullnose' 1917

Morris Eight Saloon 1938

Morris Minor convertible 1955

Morris Oxford Six Saloon 1930

Morris Minor Split Screen Panel Van (ex Royal Mail) 1958

Morris Oxford chassis 1913

Morris Oxford 1956
Morris Minor Saloon 1955
Morris Oxford Series VI 1966
Moseley JAP 1939
Norton Norton 1930
Norton Commando 1977
Norton Model 50 1963
Norton Manx 40M 1961
OK Supreme Silver Cloud 1938
Oldsmobile L-37 Sedan 1937
Oldsmobile Curved Dash 1903
Ormonde Motorcycle 1900
Packard 120 Drop Head Coupe
    1939
Paemore JAP 1950
Peugeot 106 (Electric) 1999
PJ Laydown 1985
Plymouth Prowler 1999
Pontiac Trans Am Firebird 1994
Pontiac Superior Ambulance 1968
Pontiac Trans Am Firebird 1973
Porsche 911 RS Carrera Touring
    1973
Porsche 911 Race Car 1973
Porsche 356 Coupe 1965
Porsche Boxster Roadster 1998
Porsche 111 Tractor 1953
Premier Padmini 1997
Raynard 893 Formula 3 1989
Red Bull Racing RB6 F1 2010 F1
    2010
Reliable Dayton 1909
Reliant Scimitar GTE 1974
Renault 4CV 750 1959
Renault AX 1910
Renault Caravelle convertible 1967
REVA G-Wiz 2005
Riley 1.5 Series III 1960
Riley RMA 1.5 1948
Riley Elf 1969
Riley Brooklands Special 1934

Rochdale Olympic 1968
Rochdale Olympic 1968
Rolls Royce 20HP 2 seat Drop
    Head Coupe 1928
Rolls Royce Overland Manchester
    Special 1928
Rolls Royce Phantom 1 armoured
    car replica 1929
Rolls Royce Phantom 2 Sedanca
    1930
Rolls Royce Silver Shadow II 1978
Rolls Royce Corniche 1971
Rolls Royce 40/50 Silver Ghost
    1922
Rolls Royce 20/25 Sedanca Coupe
    1932
Rotrax JAP 1976
Rotrax JAP 1979
Rover 8HP 1922
Rover 3500 Estate (prototype)
    1977
Rover 75 Saloon 1950
Rover P6 2000 1966
Rover Mini Cooper Classic 2000
Royal Enfield Royal Enfield 1962
Rudge Whitworth 1928
Saab 99 GL 1980
Scorpio GM 1980
Scott Speedway Bike 1929
Scott Clubman Special 1938
Sinclair C5 1985
Singer Gazelle 1964
Smart Smartcar 2001
Standard 10 1958
Standard Vanguard 1960
Stanley Steam Car 1921
Star Scorpio 12-25 1926
Stearns Knight 1925
Sun Wasp 1959
Sunbeam Rapier 1974
Sunbeam Rapier 1974

Sunbeam Tiger 1965
Sunbeam Talbot Mk II A 1954
Toyota MR2 1985
Trabant Saloon 600 1976
Triumph Model W 1927
Triumph 2000 Mk II 1973
Triumph Spitfire Mk3 1968
Triumph Dolomite Sprint 1978
Triumph TR3A 1957
Triumph Stag 1976
Triumph TR4A 1967
Triumph Vitesse convertible 1969
Triumph Pillarless Saloon 1933
Triumph Bonneville 1977
Triumph TR6 1975
Triumph Rocket III 2006
Triumph TR8 1981
Triumph T21 1959
Triumph T20 Tiger Cub 1959
Triumph T20 Sports Cub 1964
Triumph Trophy 1951
Trojan Cabin Cruiser 1964
Turner 950 Sports 1959
Turner Sports 1951
TVR Tuscan 1968
Ural (Irbit) Combination 2007

Van Diemen RF84 Formula Ford 1984
Vanden Plas 1300 1974
Vauxhall Victor Deluxe 1961
Vauxhall Cresta PA 1960
Velocette Mk II LE3 1967
Velocette MAC 1933
Victor Martin JAP 1930
Victor Martin Rudge 1930
Vincent Comet 1952
Volkswagen Golf GTI 1982
Volkswagen Beetle convertible 1979
Wallis Blackburn 1930
Wallis JAP 1932
Wallis-Jap 500cc ohv Wallis-Jap 1930
Weslake Antig 1984
Westfield Lotus 11 replica 1964
Westlake Antig 1976
Willys GPW Jeep 1942
Wolseley 6/80 Saloon 1950
Wolseley Hornet 1968
Wolseley 1500 1958 C
Zip Cadet (Prince Harry) 1992
Zip Cadet (Price William) 1992

HISTORY ON WHEELS MUSEUM

Common Road,
Eton Wick,
Windsor,
Berkshire, SL4 6QY, UK.
Telephone 07831 099003
Opening hours: 1000-1700 on selected days only. Check for details
www.historyonwheels.co.uk

Open since the 1970s and run by the Oliver family, this is an interesting and classic 'shed' museum that holds approximately 40 cars in a 'motors and militaria'

theme that covers cars and wartime ephemera, civilian, observer corps, transport and local history. In fact it is packed with very interesting 'stuff'. The museum holds regular open days and club meetings. Open one day a month in low season, and open for weekends and events days in high season (see website to confirm). This is a privately funded, not-for-profit concern. Recently undertaking revised 'live' exhibitions, film shows and a wartime-style cafe, it has a patio with views of Windsor Castle, with tea being served.

Of note, the museum sells original collectors' items from 1900-40 in a dedicated sales area – and these are not the usual 'repro' facsimile items; prices are accordingly realistic. Curiously, the museum also house a collection related to the late HRH Princess Diana.

Core vehicles include vintage and classic cars, military vehicles – such as General MacArthur's Cadillac, and general service vehicles. A rare Second World War 'Seep' amphibious Ford-built Jeep is also on show. 1930s displays include Mercedes-Benz cars, and military motorcycles.

With three galleries, one containing some significant military memorabilia and artefacts dating back to the Boer war, and also covering First and Second World War SOE/operations, this is an eclectic collection of vehicles, motorcycles, film-prop cars and a whole range of interesting collectors' items.

Definitely recommended as a bit of a classic gem, this is a personal and interesting private collection that whilst, (thankfully) not 'bling', is authentic and rammed to the gunwales with original and sometimes unusual items that can take several hours to study. Don't be put off by the external appearance of the building, it is well worth entering. Like so many smaller, private museums, this is a survivor and for all the right reasons. Plane-spotters will appreciate the views from the patio of departing 'heavies' from Heathrow.

IPSWICH TRANSPORT MUSEUM

Trolleybus Depot,
Cobham Road,
Ipswich,
Suffolk,
IP3 9JD, UK.
Telephone: 01473 715666

Another East Anglian gem and this one also aims for bus, and tractor enthusiasts – with Massey Ferguson and Ransomes, and David Brown history on show. The museum is a focus for tractor, implements, bus and trolley-bus enthusiasts.

ISLE OF MAN MOTOR MUSEUM (CUNNINGHAM COLLECTION)

Jurby,
Isle of Man,
IM7 3BD,UK.
Telephone: 01624 888333
www.isleofmanmotormusem.com

This privately owned, family collection created as a new museum, may be on a small and windy island off the west coast of Britain, but there is nothing small about its collection or the importance of its offering. Housed in over 70,000sqft (6,500sqm) at a former RAF airfield, the museum is just a few years old yet has already carved a niche in automotive hearts and minds on a global basis.

Note: An earlier-established Jurby Transport Museum on this RAF site was a nirvana for bus, truck and tram enthusiasts and they are not forgotten today as the museum continues is small-scale specialist niche (see below).

How many American car buffs know the Isle of Man Motor Museum is an altar to their chosen metal? Add in 1960s-70s classics, motorcycles from ancient to modern, early and late classic cars, and the fact that it is open access to all exhibits, and the ethos of this museum shines through as strongly as the light that cascades into the place – great for static photography. A dedicated motorcycle zone on the first floor caters for the two-wheeled and TT enthusiasts.

Everything from Rover P4, P6, to tanks, TVR, Maserati, MGB, Specials, Alfa Romeo, and pre-1920 motorcycles are nicely displayed across a 250 strong exhibit list which is extended by the loan of local owners' classic cars. The upper deck mezzanine floor of motorcycles represents a significant and historic collection that deserves global status.

Originally a collection started by Denis Cunningham and then extended and created by his son Darren, the Isle of Man Motor Museum is now a big production that is not to be missed if you visit the island, but also rates as a reason to visit the island itself. FYFO – fly-in-fly-out might appeal, but you would miss the stunning scenery and brilliant roads. The work of two dedicated men and team of supporters, if you are into classic cars, classic bikes, and Americana, then this place is not to be missed.

Highlights of exhibits include:

Steam Cars (including Stanley, White, and 1903 Turner-Miese)
Major American marques and examples 1950s-1970s
Lincoln Continental collection (1936, 1956, 1965)
1936 Cadillac V16
1954 GM PD-4501 Greyhound bus

Willys Jeep eight-wheel conversion
1950 Hunt three-wheeler
1953 Humber Snipe (Royal Tour car)
Facel Vega Excellence
Fiat Samantha
Amphicar
Citroen DS19 Decapotable and DS23 Tissier low-loader
European Micro cars
Motorcycle displays – 200 – veteran to modern superbikes
(note 1912 Indian, 500 Manxman, Nortons, Velocettes, Kawasakis, Hondas)
Trucks, buses, traction engines, agricultural devices.

JURBY TRANSPORT MUSEUM

Jurby,
Isle of Man,
jtm.info@manx.net

A strong collection of buses, lorries, trams, rail stock, and Manx motoring and transport memorabilia. Opened in 2010 in a refurbished historic former RAF hangar, exhibits include fire engines, heavy lorries, buses, trams, cars, and prime movers. A smaller museum but one nonetheless of importance, free entrance and charity status mean that support and donations are vital to the preservation of some unique heritage. Not to be missed, even if you are on site for the differing offer of the Isle of Man Motor Museum anyway!

LAKELAND MOTOR MUSEUM

Old Blue Mill,
Backbarrow,
Ulverston,
Cumbria, LA12 8TA. UK
Telephone 015395 30400
Opening hours: 0930-1730 daily.
www.lakelandmotormuseum.co.uk

Once known and listed in 1978 at 'Holker Hall', this now-re-sited museum and emporium (for that is what it is) dates as a museum collection from the late 1970s and is a long-established feature of the British motoring museum and ephemera scenery. It has occupied new premises in a Cumbrian mill since 2010 and is now open from May to September and boasts very rational admission prices.

The Lakeland collection contains 140 classic cars and motorcycles as well as lorries, pick-ups, aircraft and a wonderful display of memorabilia and models. The layout of the exhibits is randomly engaging and very refreshing. The museum has perhaps the largest collection of motoring memorabilia on public display in the world – with a rare collection of petrol pumps, globes, enamel advertising signs, die-cast scale models, artwork and much more. This is enamel heaven. A total of 30,000 exhibits of all categories are claimed.

The Campbell story is of course writ large (in blue) in a dedicated display hall and includes the team's blue service Land-Rover, the blue,1936 Park Ward-bodied Bentley 4½ litre, and the 1935 'Bluebird' iteration. The Bluebrid K4 and K7 boats are here too.

TVR's history is almost local so it is no surprise that the oldest surviving TVR is here.

Unlike in some museums, the vehicles are displayed in a non-linear pattern and not in ranked style. This random placing of cars creates an intimate atmosphere amid various period sets and dioramas of automobilia which work well. An upstairs gallery view also helps. Definitely an imaginative and thought-about presentation and a top Cumbrian attraction amid many that vie for attention.

A special display in tribute to the Isle of Man Tourist Trophy (TT) charts the history of this legendary motorcycle race with a hall of fame, video displays and timeline tracing its history from 1907.

For motorcyclists, the 'must see' Vincent display includes the Black Shadow, Comet, Rapide, and the Black Lightning, and tells the story of the company's founder Philip Conrad Vincent and his mission to influence the world of motorcycling. Also exhibited is the only surviving Braithwaite motorcycle of around twenty built by brothers Bert and Jack Braithwaite in their works at Staveley, north of Kendal. The brothers designed and built what must be one of the world's first over-head valved motorcycle engines (1906); the pushrods were converted to a crossover design in 1912 which greatly improved power output and efficiency. The motorcycle was constantly updated to the early 1950s. Further exhibits include the Campbell family land speed and water speed vehicles and team support items and memorabilia. There are over 100 motorcycles and scooters and the collection traces the development of some classic British marques from performance bikes to cultural icons.

Known over the years for the loan and exhibition of some interesting veteran and vintage cars, the Lakeland remains an old friend, an up-close and personal motoring experience and one to be treasured for that, yet which has moved with the times in the new age of the museum. A top tier rating is obvious. The enthusiasm is tangible. Enamel and petroleum artefacts fans need to stay a while here and just sigh. Serial fettlers can gaze through the restoration workshop window.

Lakeland is highly recommended for a superb full day out – it is indeed a 'petrol-head's' passion.

LLANGOLLEN MOTOR MUSEUM

Pentre Felin Mill,
Llangollen,
Denbighshire,
LL20 8EE, Wales
Telephone: 01978 860 324
Opening hours: 0930-1700 Friday-Monday
www.llangollenmotormuseum.com

A true, old fashioned, family run museum in old building, full of charm, personal touches and real classic car enthusiasm.

There are 60-plus car and motorcycles. Most are runners. Exhibits include a Model T Ford, Vauxhall 14/40, and examples of Austin, Citroën, and Triumph and a nice array of interesting classic British motorcycles; all set out in a large hall, packed with memorabilia, it provides family fun, and is dog friendly! Cheap to enter and worth lingering over, a Triumph TR4 is the museum's star car. This place has true charm and old-fashioned motoring appeal. Well worth the visit and much loved it seems.

LANCHESTER MUSEUM, LIBRARY & ARCHIVE

Frederick Lanchester Library,
Coventry University,
Gosford Street,
Coventry,
CV1 5DD, UK.
Monday to Friday 1000-1700. Saturday & Sunday 1000-1600
www.lanchesterinteractivearchive.org

The Lanchester Museum/ Interactive Archive is based on the second floor of Coventry University's Frederick Lanchester Library. The university was in its early days known as the 'Lanchester Polytechnic'. The University hosts one of the world's top car design courses and the superb Lanchester museum and interactive resource tributes Sir Frederick Lanchester – one of Britain's greatest engineers and designers. Tagged as 'Britain's Leonardo da Vinci', Lanchester created advanced engineering and inventions from the late 1800s onwards, he was a pioneer in many fields including that of elliptical wing design, transmissions and aerodynamics.

Lanchester is perhaps best known for designing and building the first all-British motor car in 1895 but he also published papers and books detailing the first scientific principles of flight, and theorised about the principles of colour photography before it was reality, and devised military strategies that underpin business management courses still taught today. Now headed by Antony Hughes, the Lanchester Interactive Archive project and Coventry University, are indebted to the dedication of Chris Clark, Lanchester Historian, for his support to Coventry University over many years, and his perseverance to bring the archive of Frederick Lanchester to a wider, appreciative audience.

Highly recommended, and truly educational, this place is a true 'hidden gem' and deserving of support and wider recognition. Give them an award someone!

Readers and car clubs are advised to book ahead if possible.

LINCOLNSHIRE ROAD TRANSPORT MUSEUM

(Lincolnshire Vintage Vehicle Society)
Whisby Road,
North Hykeham,
Lincolnshire,
LN63QT, UK.
Opening: Summer (May-October) Monday-Friday 1100-1600. Open Sunday not Saturday. Winter Sundays only 1300-1600.
www.lvvs.org.uk

Here on a site started in the 1960s and rehoused in a new building in 1993 and with new building in 2010, can be found 65 vintage and classic vehicles including cars, and some notable buses and commercials. Numerous displays and memorabilia are on show in what is a classic, vital local museum of its type. Privately run by the Lincolnshire Vintage Vehicle Society Ltd (founded 1959) as a registered charity and based at the museum, this is a true enthusiasts' haven. Sadly, the workshop is not generally open to public – which perhaps might make a new attraction for committed and knowledgeable enthusiasts if it was.

The museum/society website is excellent and details vehicles and restorations and can be used to plan your visit. The museum hosts an annual transport festival in April and also organises a classic vehicle rally every summer, as well as 'Open days' at Easter and in November.

Bus fans will like the 1940 Bristol L5G single deck and 1949 K5G double decker. Cars include:

1930s Austin Sevens
1981 Allegro
1975 Enfield
1969 Ford Capri
1966 Hillman Super Minx Estate
1966 Rover 2000
1930 Singer Junior
1939 SS Jaguar 2.5 saloon
1946 Standard Flying 12
1937 Vauxhall 12.

Also features the 'Delaine' bus company, a Lincolnshire bus service company with well over 100 years of local history to its credit.

Motorcycles include 1950s and 1960s classics of AJS, Honda, Mobylette, Puch, Raleigh, Trojan, and Velocette marques.

The bus collection covers 35 interesting vehicles of AEC, Bristol, Leyland, and Daimler marques. Commercials includes 13 vehicles of AEC, Albion, Bedford, Dennis Leyland, Morris and Reliant, all dated 1934 to 1953.

With interesting vehicles, cycles, models, numerous displays, transport and local memorabilia, on-going projects, and knowledgeable staff, the true enthusiast and restoration addict could easily spend more than half a day here. The Lincolnshire Road Transport Museum (an accredited museum since 2009) is what it is meant to be – does what it says on the tin and is a refreshing, no-thrills offering. More *Practical Classics* and *Classic Bus* than something of upmarket octane rating, it is a museum where the motoring and transport enthusiast can really get in touch with a colourful and interesting engineering past. Highly recommended for the enthusiast and yet also unlikely to put off children needing educating into British engineering history. Without doubt this museum is an important resource and record amid our national motoring museums movement.

LONDON BUS PRESERVATION TRUST (MUSEUM)

Cobham Hall, Brooklands Museum,
Brooklands Road,
Weybridge, Surrey, KT13 0QN, UK.
www.londonbusmuseum.com

The London Bus Preservation Trust and its museum is dedicated to preserving and restoring its collection of historic London buses and having moved from

its former London home, has since 2011, been based in the Cobham Hall at Brooklands Museum.

Not surprisingly, this is the largest collection of working historic London buses in the world; 35 buses and coaches representing the great era of British bus, coach building, chart a history of chassis and body construction that goes back many decades – 1875 to 1980.

Items of street furniture and other artefacts and memorabilia related to bus operations in London are also on display, from uniforms to ticket machines, medals, signs and examples of the famous 1930s-60s posters-as-works-of-art for which London Transport received many awards

MALDON MUSEUM OF POWER

Hatfield Road, Langford,
Maldon, Essex, CM9 6QA, UK.
Telephone: 01621 8443183
opening hours: 100-1600. Wednesday to Sundays

Although not strictly a motoring museum, this is a museum of undoubted interest to anyone of mechanical persuasion and preservation. There are engines, cars and artefacts on show, local classic car clubs make regular club day out visits. 'TransportFest', 'Bikemeet', 'American Car Show' and a 'Coffee & Cars' on the fourth Sunday of the month, are all regular or annual events. Themed, and marque-specific car shows, exhibitions, steam events, model and toy fairs, and weekend events all take place at the museum. A camp site makes staying over for such events an easy process if you are on a budget.

Running privately for over 20 years and with recent National Lottery funding, the Museum of Power is reinventing itself not just as a preservation point, but also a local resource for recreation, learning and community engagement – as so many smaller museums have had to adapt to in a changing museum environment.

Run by a small team, a new entrance building and facilities are planned. Housed in a former water pumping station, the museum contains a diverse collection of engines used for pumping and industrial processes. The Lilleshal Company Ltd triple expansion steam pump is a working engine of great rarity and takes pride of place. Diesel engines, a display of 'Eco' cars and design prototypes are noteworthy. A miniature light railway also runs on site.

This is definitely an example of a small museum run by a dedicated team who work hard to ensure its viability and attraction. We might even rate it a gem of an engine shed!

Key exhibits:

Lillehal Steam Pump
Paxman twin-cylinder horizontal engine
Eco-cars
Steam Turbines
Valves
Dawson and Downe steam pump
Bellis and Morgan Birmingham Pump
Steam engines
Diesel engines

MANX TRANSPORT HERITAGE MOTOR MUSEUM

Mill Road,
Peel,
Isle of Man, IM 5 1TB, UK.
Telephone 01624 842448
Open weekends

At less than 100sqm this is possibly a minnow of a museum but one covering Manx motoring and the infamous Peel P50 single-seater micro car that was built locally in 1964. If you are on the island, then why miss it, even if the visit will be short.

MILESTONES MUSEUM

Basingstoke Leisure Park,
Churchill Way,
Basingstoke RG22 6PG, UK.
Telephone: 01256 639550
Open Tuesday- Friday 1000-1645. Open weekends, closed Monday.

Opened in 2000, and although not a 'pure' motoring museum, this place is packed with transport history via commercials, fire engines, lorries, vans, and locally-related transport memorabilia. Recreated streets of old England also feature.

Taskers, Wallis & Stevens, and Thornycroft are all well represented as local Hampshire vehicle builders and mechanical engineers. Steam-driven Thornycroft on display. Records car manufacture in Basingstoke 1903-1912.

Trams, buses, motorcycles and agricultural engineering all feature in a period setting. Also features many original and traditional commercial histories and buildings. Has a good cafe and is ideal for a family visit. Commercial vehicle enthusiasts will not be disappointed.

MORAY MOTOR MUSEUM

Bridge Street,
Elgin,
IV30 4DE,
Scotland.
Telephone: 01343 544933
Opening hours: 1100-1700 daily. Seasonal.
www.moraymotormuseum.org

Contains, veteran, vintage, classic cars, motorcycles, models and automobilia. Often rated as 'excellent', this out-the-way museum packs a punch in a soft glove of presentation and context. Walk in and see a rare Bristol sports-bodied type, or a Jensen 541R. Early Edwardian cars such as a 1904 Speedwell and the 1910 Daimler Tourer are here; so too is a lovely blue 1921 Regent Sport motorcycle that certainly catches the enthusiast's eye. Bentleys, Jaguars, a 1929 Rolls-Royce Phantom and of note a nice 1937 BMW 328, as well as 1951 Frazer Nash, and a rare 1954 Lagonda V12, can all also can be seen.
   Contents include:

Bristol
Jaguar
Aston Martin
Nash
Lotus
Lister-Jaguar
Ferrari
MG
Riley
Austin
bubble cars
modern classics

Enthusiast rated, yet also family friendly, the people that run this museum know their stuff and you can see why people say it is Scotland's leading motor museum. Highly recommended.

MURRAYS MOTORCYCLE MUSEUM

Santon Villa, Santon,
Isle of Man, IM4 1EN, UK.
Telephone: 01624 823223

Is this one of the best men-in-sheds museums ever? It could well be. A fascinating place, packed to the rafters with motorcycles, memorabilia, and sheer, tangible love for motorcycles, this museum reeks of the authentic and the personal. It pays little service to modern philosophical theories of the new museum culture, yet succeeds as a brilliant, must-visit for the true and perhaps slightly older motorcycle maniac. This is a place to come for visit, a cuppa, and a chat about times past and times fast. Possibly not the place for shiny, digital, corporate-speak people though!

Now run by the founder's son, the museum is privately funded and is based 'at home'. As such it has returned to its beginnings when it began as a small personal collection. In its mid-life, a dedicated building housed the ever growing museum and TT-tribute collection, which included some very rare motorcycles. An original Honda machine was gifted to the museum by Mr S. Honda himself when he toured the Isle of Man decades ago. Yet so rare was the motorcycle that Honda asked the museum if they would release it back to the Honda collection in Japan – which the Murray museum did.

Having re-organised and restocked, the museum is now back in a 'home' location that some might find less than fashionably 'bling'. This place is about machines not marketing. A place to revel in old motorcycles and artefacts with aroma! A very large, man-shed then.

MUSEUM OF LINCOLN LIFE

Old Barracks, Burton Road,
Lincoln, LN1 3LY, UK.
Opening hours: 1000-1600 selected days.
www.visitlincoln.com

Agricultural and vintage machinery exhibited in a small but very visitable museum. Tractors, tractions, steamers, threshers, and all manner or lovely old artefacts. Nostalgia on stooks and recommended for the enthusiast. Serves great cake – as every museum should.

MUSEUM OF LIVERPOOL (TRANSPORT)

Pier Head,
Liverpool Waterfront,
Liverpool,
L3 1DG, UK.
Telephone: 0151 478 4545

Ford, and other car makers have made cars and car engines in Liverpool. Liverpool Speke airport was an early cog in British domestic action prior to 1939. So a healthy transport section at the Museum of Liverpool and its recently built waterfront home should be no surprise. They like cars and motorcycles in Liverpool (and ships, the maritime museum is nearby).

Intriguingly, Liverpool once boasted a 'Lark Lane Motor Museum'. This is now a recording studio. Some of the Lark Lane Museum's cars were dispersed to the Wirral Transport Museum after the Liverpool city museum declined the Lark Lane's owner's offer and terms. The Lark Lane Museum (off Hesketh Street), was a true enthusiasts' 'oily rag' emporium with, it seems, an owner (Jim) with a penchant for Lancias and Italian classic metal of four and two-wheeled types.

The first modern mass-production car made on Merseyside was a Ford Anglia from Halewood and that very car is in the museum of Liverpool's transport collection – where 200 vehicles from cars to trams and commercials are held.

Also on site are the 1920s Liverpool-made AER motorcycle, traction engines, horse-drawn devices, bicycles, Leyland fire engines, railway locomotives, trams, and the 1900 'Liver' Lea Motor Company 3½hp car. The locally built 1910 Vulcan 15hp car with 'Doctor's Victoria' coachwork is a very rare sight for the Edwardian era car fancier. Liverpool's overhead railway heritage is also displayed.

Another superb transport section museum within a larger museum network: recommended.

MUSEUM OF TRANSPORT MANCHESTER (GMTS)

Boyle Street, Cheetham,
Manchester, M8 8UW, UK.
Telephone 0181 205 2122
Opening hours: 1000-1630. See website for variances and events.
www.gmts.co.uk

Established in 1977 and operating since 1979, this is a public transport and commercial vehicle orientated collection that focuses on operations in the Manchester and north west region. A volunteer-run museum with close ties to the Greater Manchester Transport Society (GMTS) which operates and staffs the museum.

One of the largest such collections in the UK, not all its 80-plus collection of vehicles are held on site due to storage constraints. Housed in a former bus garage dating from the 1920s, this creates an evocative and tangible atmosphere of past lives and great authenticity.

A highlight is that the restoration area and works are accessible to visitors – a key ingredient in engagement and promoting interest for enthusiasts. Many of the buses are drivable and fully working. Trams dating from 1901 are also on show, and an extensive archive collection is of note. Classic buses from AEC, Bristol, Daimler, Atkinson, Crossley, Guy, Seddon, and Leyland are all in evidence.

Exhibits include:

Manchester horse drawn buses from 1890
South Lancashire Tramways, Brush Tram 1906
Motor buses from all the main regional operators and private companies dating from 1920s-1980s.
Coaches from local private operators 1947-1975.
Trolleybuses 1950's.
Electric buses 1975
Light Rail 1990s.
Ancillary vehicles 1920s-1940s.

For the bus enthusiast, this is another top-rated classic emporium. Cheap to enter, full of interesting vehicles and memorabilia, and crucially a 'working' museum with many 'live' buses. Worth hopping off at.

MYRETON MOTOR MUSEUM

Aberlady,
Longniddry,
East Lothian
EH32 0PZ,
Scotland.
Telephone: 01875 870288
Opening hours: 1030-1630 daily

Opened as far back as 1966 by the late W. Dale, Myreton occupies interesting old building on the Lothian coast and is a bit draughty say some! After Beaulieu

and some bigger names, this is one of the oldest continuously operating motor museums in the UK. It is very authentic and much admired. We might call it a thoroughbred museum – if somewhat vintage.

There are three halls of interesting and eclectic cars (totalling over 30) spanning from 1899 through the twentieth century up to modern classics era of the Fiat X19.

Exhibits include:

**Citroen Traction
Avant
Jaguar XJ6
Fiat 500
1919 Model TT commercial
Ford with special charabanc body
Morris Minor
Vauxhalls
1930s MGs.**

Memorabilia and a good collection of enamel signs complement an eclectic range of cars. But the website is not particularly easy to use. However, this is an enjoyable and interesting museum that does what is has always said on the tin.

Above: Sammy Miller MBE – the motorcycle man who really is a bit of a legend and so his his superb museum. Here he welcomes the newly acquired Zundapp to the museum. (Photo: SMM)

Below: The National Motor Cycle Museum (NMM) began as a personal collection and is now a world-class international shrine for 'bikers' and motor cycle enthusiasts. (Photo: NMM)

Above: 1949 Norton 500cc. Geoff Duke. Legendary stuff at the NMM. (Photo: NMM)

Below: 1949 Vincent Black Shadow Series C at the NMM. Just simply stare. (Photo: NMM)

Above: Rotaries in action on the track at the NMM. You can ride a classic motorcycle here. (Photo: NMM)

Below: It's gold and its gripping. Brough being very superior. (Photo: NMM)

Above: Rhone classic seen at a French museum.

Left: Indian in blue. Classic bikes make such a sight and have a huge following.

Above: Racer Bill Little (seated) and his wonderful personal collection of motorcycles and memorabilia housed in a barn. Now closed.

Right: Signs are all the rage. These are of their time and not politically correct or acceptable by modern standards, but they are old.

Bugattis gathered at an evocative Prescott in a time-warp of nostalgia.

1930s Alfa Romeo Tipo B hastens up the hill at Prescott. Old cars must be driven, especially a racer like this.

Above: Allard P-series captured at a private collection. A curious 1950s British car but classic to its core.

Below: Ford low-rider, Americana. Another facet of the old car enthusiasm. Can't you just hear it burble.

Above: Old British steel at rest. The authentic aura of British classics. Not an interactive display in sight!

Left: Ford Thunderbird patina as the car awaits restoration at an American private collection.

Right: A Rolls-Royce and a Supermarine S-Series float-pane racer mascot! Utterly classic stuff.

Below: This 1930s Buick drove 150,000 miles in per-war Asia at the hands of its titled owner who owned the Tate and Lyle sugar empire. It survived the war and came back to Britain.

Above: Its that Japanese classic again — the fascinating Datsun Fairlady alongside one its major influences — the Triumph Spitfire. Fairlady was successful in the USA, but not in Europe. Was it Michelotti-styled — like its Triumph rival?

Opposite: VW high-roof and autojumble offerings seen in France at the Loheac Museum autobrocante.

The Voskhod, a rare Russian motorcycle of robust 'workhorse' engineering. Marketed in the UK in the 1970s as 'Cossack' motorcycles. Another surprising sight at a small museum.

On the move, Warwick of Michigan 1899-1905: proper veteran motoring.

A V12 Jaguar E-Type and a Bristol Britannia at the Bristol Collection. Capturing the essence of classic British mechanicals.

The prototype 2CV seen in its original 'barn find' attic location where it was discovered. (Photo: Citroën)

Saab's flying saucer of a car, the 92 Prototype at the Saab Museum. (Photo: Saab)

P 92001

Amphicar emerges from a Loheac Museum's lake during 'drive it day'.

BMW's amazing 1930s 328, a landmark in car design and motorsport. JMP 5 is in fact the Frazer Nash BMW version of the model.

Opposite: Alpine Renaults gather at Loheac Museum, France. Plastique fantastique.

NATIONAL MOTOR MUSEUM BEAULIEU (THE)

Beaulieu,
Brockenhurst,
Hampshire, SO42 7ZN, UK.
Telephone: 01590 612345. NMM Trust: 01590 614650
Opening hours: 1000-1700/1800 daily/seasonal: see website
www.beaulieu.co.uk

'I have always believed that Britain's great houses and gardens, originally created for the pleasure of a few, should now be enjoyed by the many. I am also dedicated to ensuring that the story of Britain's motoring heritage should be appreciated by the widest possible audience.'

Edward, Lord Montagu of Beaulieu (1926-2015)

The vital cog in the establishment and development of the motor museum in our society, yet one that has indeed moved with the times and reinvigorated itself and its offering over many years, the National Motor Museum (formerly the Douglas-Scott-Montagu) offers true automotive diversity, from an Allard dragster to a rare veteran car collection. Motorsport is well covered as are all the ages and aspects of our cars and our motoring. Reflecting John Douglas-Scott-Montagu's Edwardian era interest in cars, his son Edward created the original collection in the 1950s. Upon his passing, the family and the current title-holder continue to guide this significant hub in the motoring world, on its future course.

This is a truly world class museum that tells so many stories, yet never feels too 'marketing'. Beaulieu auto jumble is of course world famous and now twice-yearly. The collections and displays are diverse and valuable across all the eras of the car. So much time and effort has gone into the creation of the museum over the years and it is so good to see that whilst it has moved with the times, it has not lost its soul or ethos – this is still car and motorcycle heaven. The contents are regularly driven and ridden.

New themes and new museum culture may be apparent, but Beaulieu remains a must see experience, and a deep one at that. They also serve proper cake!

The motorsport sections and displays pay fine tribute to British motorsport across its story from Edwardian pioneers through to 21st century F1 cars.

'Grand Prix Greats' celebrates the history of F1, whilst 'Road, Race & Rally' focuses on sports cars from rallying, hill-climbing, and the consumer market.

Key motorsport exhibits include:

1903 Napier Gordon Bennett. One of the oldest British racing cars.

1912 Sunbeam 3-Litre is one of five cars built by Sunbeam for the 1912 Coupe de l'Auto at Dieppe, the first of many successful international races for Sunbeam.

1924 Bugatti Type 35. Perhaps the most famous of all Bugatti models, the Type 35 and its derivatives dominated motor racing for much of the 1920s.

1950 BRM V16. Made famous during its heyday driven by motorsport aces Juan Manuel Fangio and Reg Parnell, only five examples of this pioneering British design were built. Although ultimately unsuccessful, the BRM was a stepping stone on the path to Britain's dominance of the sport in later years.

1967 Lotus 49. The first car to use the legendary Ford-Cosworth DFV engine, setting new standards for Grand Prix racers.

Williams - Renault (Damon Hill) FW18 1996. A defining car in Formula 1 and Williams history.

Rally cars include the 1981 Ford Escort RS 1800, driven by Ari Vatanen in the 1981 RAC Rally, the year in which he won the Drivers' Championship.

A real rarity is the 1961 Allard Chrysler Dragster – Britain's first dragster and part of Sydney Allard's amazing story. The car attracted huge interest and its popularity helped spark the establishment of the British Drag Racing Association. American dragster aces toured the UK with Sydney Allard and helped establish the British dragster movement in the 1960s.

The Caravan and Motorhome Club Collection contains over a century of archival material and memorabilia from one of Europe's premier touring organisations.

The Shell Heritage Art Collection is one of the most important collections of commercial art in the world, featuring the work of well-known British artists from the 1900s to the 1980s.

Key motor cycle exhibits include:

1903 Triumph. Believed to be oldest Triumph in existence.

1912 Norton BS ('Old Miracle'). One of the most famous Norton racing motor cyles. This example was particularly associated with Daniel 'Wizard' O'Donovan, the first rider to exceed 80mph on a 500cc bike.

1919 Royal Enfield experimental 4-cylinder. Despite excellent performance, this experimental prototype was cancelled due to high production costs.

1928 Rudge Whitworth. Ridden to victory by Graham Walker in the 1928 Ulster Grand Prix.

1954 Norton prototype 250cc. An experimental high-camshaft, overhead-valve prototype.

1955 Vincent Black Shadow. One of the last motorcycles to carry the famous Vincent name.

1961 Honda RC162. Ridden to victory by Mike Hailwood in the 1961 TT, this design heralded the beginning of Japanese domination of motorcycle racing.

1975 Kawasaki. Mick Grant's 1975 Isle of Man Senior TT-winning bike.

1979 Honda CBX 1000. Widely regarded as one of the most impressive motorcycles of all time. At the time of launch it was the fastest and most powerful road bike in the world.

The Motoring Archives represent a variety of records illustrative of motoring history. Material is held in support of the National Motor Museum Trust's wider collections, as well as providing a rich resource via the Motoring Research Service. The archives are largely paper-based and include material relating to business, trade associations, and personalities. There are approximately 300 collections, an estimated 100,000 items housed in over 1,000 boxes, equating to 24 cubic metres.

Cataloguing work is ongoing; a partially complete catalogue, listing several key collections held by the Motoring Archives, can be found on the Archives Hub, a national online database for archival collections.

Car clubs, magazines, television programmes and a range of motoring themes visit and occur at Beaulieu.

The entry fee to Beaulieu is good value when one considers the totality of the offering on the Beaulieu site and the full day out that is on offer..

The National Motor Museum is of course brilliant and highly recommended and is in many ways, a world leader. It caters for the forensic classic car or motorsport sleuth, the dedicated enthusiast, and the family visitor. It educates a new generation into our motoring history and it really is a super day out. Homemade cake and local ale are served.

All Beaulieu needs to add is a classic, Erik Carlsson, Saab rally display (Erik married Stirling Moss's sister Pat, a famed rally driver who herself deserves a tribute display too) and the couple lived in England, so an honorary statue and an

old Saab (as built using many British-designed components and engineered by a British-trained engineer) would be good.

Beaulieu main vehicle contents list:

ABC Skootamota 1920
AC Model 70 1976
AC Shelby Cobra 1965
Acrostar BD-5J Jet 1983
AEC Regent MkIII RT Double
   Decker Bus 1950
AJS 7R 1958
AJS Model 16M 1946
Albion A14 1914
Allard Dragster 5.8 1960
Allard J2 1950
Alvis Speed 25 1937
AMC Hornet 1974
Argyll 15/30 hp 1913
Ariel Chopper 1954
Ariel Leader 1959
Ariel Square Four 1931
Ariel Tricycle 1898
Ascot–Pullin Utility De Luxe 1930
Aston Martin 1.5-litre 1922
Aston Martin DB5 1963
Aston Martin DB5 1964
Aston Martin DBS 2008
Aston Martin DBS 2006
Aston Martin DBS Stunt Car 2006
Aston Martin DBS with
   continuity damage 2008
Aston Martin V12 Vanquish 2002
Aston Martin V8 Volante 1984
ATCO Trainer 1939
Auburn 851 1935
Audi Quattro A2 Rally Car 1983
Austin 20 hp Breakdown Truck
   1926
Austin A40 Farina 1966
Austin A40 Somerset 1953
Austin A90 Atlantic 1952
Austin Clifton 12/4 1928

Austin Healey 100M 1956
Austin Mini Cooper S Downton
   1963
Austin Mini Seven 1959
Austin Seven Swallow 1932
Austin Seven Tourer 1928
Austin Seven Tourer 1923
BAT 5/6 hp With Sidecar 1913
Bath-O-Sub 1971
Bayliss Thomas 1928
Bean Short 14 1928
Bedford Cadbury Crème Egg
   1989
Bell-Textron Jet Pack 2002
Benelli 750 Sei 1978
Benelli Adiva Scooter
Bentley 4.5 Litre Supercharged
   1930
Benz (Replica) 1886
Benz Velo 1898
Bluebird CN7 1961
BMW 750iL 1997
BMW Isetta 300 Super Plus 1962
BMW R1200C 1997
BMW R50 With Steib Sidecar 1957
BMW Z8 1999
Bolster Special Bloody Mary 1929
Bombardier MX Z-Rev Ski-Doo
   2002
BRM 1.5 litre V16 Type 15 MkI
   1950
Brockhouse Corgi Scooter 1949
Brough Superior 11.50 Special
   Combination 1936
Brush Pony 1947
BSA B25 2 hp 1925
BSA Bantam D1 1949
BSA M21 1960

BSA S28 OHV 1928
BSA Victor Grand Prix Works
  Scrambler 1967
Bugatti Type 15 1910
Bugatti Type 35 1924
Burial-At-Sea Bed 1967
Cadillac Model A 1903
Cagiva 600 W16 1995
Calcott 11.9 hp 1923
Caterham SP/300R 2011
Cello Case Sled 1985
Chevrolet Aveo 2012
Chitty Chitty Chitty Bang Bang
Citroën 2CV 1981
Citroen 2CV6 Special 1986
Citroen Xsara WRC 2005
Columbia Electric 1901
Commer Auto-Sleeper 1964
Connaught B-Type 1955
Cooper 500 MkIII 1949
Cord 810 Westchester Sedan 1937
Coventry Eagle B33 1926
Crocodile Mini-Sub 1983
Crossley Burney Streamline 1934
Daimler 22 hp 1903
Daimler Bottle Lorry 1924
Daimler 12 hp 1899
Daimler Cannstatt 1898
Damon Hill's Williams - Renault
  FW18 1996
Datsun Type 14 Saloon 1935
De Dietrich 24 hp 1903
De Dion-Bouton Model Q 6 hp
  1904
De Dion-Bouton Model Q 6 hp
  1903
DeLorean Motor Company
  DeLorean DMC-12 1981
Del Boy's Reliant Regal 1971
Dixon-Bate Trailer 1932
Douglas Model R 1913

Douglas Vespa 152/L2 1959
Douglas With Dixon Banking
  Sidecar 1923
Ducati 998R 2002
Durkopp Diana 1957
Eccles Caravan 1926
Elstar Jap Grasstrack 1948
Fairey Marine Huntress Speedboat
  1962
Ferrari Dino 246 GT 1974
Fiat 3.5 hp 1899
Fiat Tipo Zero 1913
Ford Anglia 105E 'Flying Car'
  1966
Ford Anglia E494A 1949
Ford Capri 1600L 1971
Ford Consul Convertible MkI
  1955
Ford Consul Cortina MkI 1963
Ford Escort RS Rally Car 1981
Ford Ka 2008
Ford Model T 1914
Ford Model T Van 1914
Ford Model Y 1937
Ford Mustang Mach 1 1971
Ford Thunderbird 2002
Ford V8 Utility 1937
Ford Sierra RS Cosworth 1986
Frazer Nash Colmore 1932
Glastron Carlson CV-23HT 1978
Glastron GT-150 1973
Gobron-Brillié Fire Engine 1907
Golden Arrow 1929
Graham Hill's Lotus 49 R3 1967
Grégoire 12CV 1905
Greeves Hawkstone 1961
Grenville Steam Carriage 1880
Harley-Davidson 11 hp 1915
Harley-Davidson 42 WLC 1942
Harrods Electric Van 1939
Healey Elliot 2.4 litre 1947

Hillman Imp De Luxe Saloon 1963
Hillman Minx Magnificent 1938
Hispano-Suiza Alfonso XIII 1912
Honda RC162 1961
Honda ATC 1971
Honda CB750KO 1970
Honda CBR 900 Fireblade 1996
Honda Supersport CBX1000 1979
Humber 8 hp 1909
Ice Dragster 2002
Itala 120 hp 1907. Winner of the
   1907 Coppa della Velocita driven
   by Alessandro Cagno.[1][2]
Jaguar E-Type 3.8 1962
Jaguar XK150 3.8 Litre 1960
Jaguar XKR Convertible 2002
Jensen Interceptor 1969
Jowett Javelin 1949
Kawasaki Factory Racer 1975
Knight 1895
Lambretta B Scooter 1948
Lambretta LD 150 Scooter 1957
Lambretta Li 150 1966
Land Rover R.04 1948
Lotus 78 John Player Special
   16 1977
Lotus Esprit S1 1977
Lotus JPS Europa 1973
Lotus (Graham Hill's) 49 R3 1967
M & L Trials Special 1954
Matchless 2½hp 1905
Maxwell 25cwt Charabanc 1922
McLaren Honda MP4/4-6 1988
McLaren Mercedes MP4/21 2010
Mercedes 60 hp 1903
Mercury Cougar XR7 1969
MG M-Type 1930
MG PA 1935
MG MGC GT 1968
Michael Schumacher's Ferrari
   F310 V10 Replica 1996

Mini Outspan Orange 1972
Mobil Pup 1919
Montesa Cota 4RT 2008
Morgan Aero-Sports 1927
Morris 1000 Post Office Van 1970
Morris 8 Series II 4-Door Saloon
   1938
Morris Cowley Bullnose 1924
Morris Minor 1949
Morris Minor SV 2 Seater 1931
Morris Minor Traveller 1970
Morris Mobile Grocery Shop 1933
Motosacoche 2.5 hp 1913
Mr Bean's Mini 1979
Napier Gordon Bennett 1903
Ner-A-Car 1921
Norton 16H 1942
Norton 30M Manx 1960
Norton Commando 1975
Norton Dominator 1954
Norton Jubilee 250cc 1961
Norton Prototype 1953
Norton BS 1912
NSU 3HP 1906
Osprey Hovercraft 2002
Parachute 1964
Parahawk 1999
Peel P50 1964
Pennington Autocar 1896
Perks and Birch Autowheel
   1899
Peter Ustinov's Mercedes 36/220
   1928
Peters 2¾hp 1924
PIG (Pipeline Inspection Gauge)
   1985
Pope-Tribune 6 hp 1904
Q Jet Boat 1999
Reliant 6cwt Van 1947
Reliant Regal MkI 1953
Renault 11 TXE 1985

Renault 14/20 hp XB 1906
Renault 1¾hp 1899
Riley 1.5 Litre TT Sprite 1936
Riley Falcon 1934
Rolls-Royce 40/50 Phantom I 1925
Rolls-Royce Alpine Eagle 1914
Rolls-Royce Phantom III 1937
Rolls-Royce Phantom VI 1970
Rolls-Royce Silver Cloud II 1962
Rolls-Royce Silver Shadow II 1977
Rolls-Royce Silver Shadow MkI
   1968
Rolls-Royce Silver Ghost 1909
Rotrax Jap Speedway 1950
Rover Rover 14 1938
Rover P4 1963
Rover P6 (2000) 1967
Royal Caravan 1955
Royal Enfield 3 hp 1914
Royal Enfield Crusader 1959
Royal Enfield Experimental 1919
Royal Enfield Prototype Army
   Mod 1945
Royal Enfield Quadricycle 1900
Rudge-Whitworth 1928
Sinclair C5 1985

Skyfleet S570 model 2006
Solar Flair 1993
Speargun Sled 1977
Standard Vanguard Saloon 1951
Sunbeam 16 hp 1914
Sunbeam 350 hp 1920
Sunbeam 1000 hp 1927
Sunbeam Coupe De L'Auto 1912
Sunbeam Cub 1924
Sunbeam Standard Model 3
   1924
Sunbeam-Talbot 90 1952
Surfboard 2002
Talbot 105 1934
Top Methanol Dragster 1994
Tow Sled 1965
Triumph 2.5HP 1903
Triumph 3TW 1940
Triumph 5T Speed Twin 1948
Triumph 6T Thunderbird 1949
Triumph Bonneville T120R 1962
Triumph Herald Saloon 1960
Triumph Trident T150 1972
Triumph TR2 1954
Williams - Renault (Damon Hill)
   FW18 1996

NATIONAL MOTORCYCLE MUSEUM

Coventry Road, Bickenhill,
Solihull, West Midlands,
B92 0EJ, UK.
Opening hours:
Telephone: 01675 443311
www.

1,000 British motorcycles of all eras and types populate this vital museum. This superb resource was set up as a family business in the mid-1980s by W.R. 'Roy' Richards and is now run as a Trust by his family. From a private collection to a

leading world-class museum is a huge achievement and the museum's aim is to preserve the British motorcycle history for future generations, as a reminder of Britain's industry and engineering prowess.

The 'Friends of the National Motorcycle Museum' is a new and important scheme that allows the funds to be created to preserve the legacy of the collection and to offer unique experiences to visitors. For a reasonable fee, anyone (almost) can be tutored and actually ride a vintage/classic motorcycle on site – great stuff for grumpy old men with fond memories of their youths. The Friends' scheme offers several great days out and activities.

The National Motorcycle Museum is generally recognised as the leading motorcycle museum in the UK and the most significant, largest British motorcycle museum and collection in the world.

In its original iteration, it opened its doors in October 1984 with a collection of 350 motorcycles on display. The Museum owes its formation to the drive and ambition of Roy Richards. Roy died in 2008 but his work continues under the guardianship of his widow Christine and sons Simon and Nick, with the museum collection now boasting some 1,000-plus machines, most fully restored to the manufacturers' original specifications.

Since opening, this magnificent centre has become the largest motorcycle museum in the world and attracts around 250,000 visitors a year. One of the biggest attractions for many guests is the comprehensive cross-section of British machines, spanning the great years of motorcycle manufacturing in the UK. With machines of all types and marques from the earliest veterans through to the powerful 650cc 'twins', all the motorcycles are displayed in numerical/year order 1898-1960 and the display also includes the museum's large collection of both Vincent & Sunbeam machines.

A key highlight for the 'vintagent' is the 1913-14 Matchless V-Twin Works Racer – a unique V-Twin Brooklands/TT Works Racer of which only around half a dozen were ever made in the period before the First World War; this is the only surviving example and was restored 2015-18 by the museum's chief restorer, Colin Wall, who declared it 'the most difficult restoration I have ever attempted'.

Many classic bike enthusiasts will have spent an afternoon browsing through the museum's halls, and numerous clubs and organisations having held rallies and events in the grounds. The National Motorcycle Museum has developed into a focal point for the British Motorcycle movement. It is conveniently located in the heart of the Midlands transport network, with Birmingham International railway station just a five-minute taxi ride away – although a brisk walk might be quicker on heavy traffic days! I stayed and parked nearby in Warwick and took a local train to the museum via Birmingham International – quick, cheap, environmentally advisable and very easy.

NMM also contains the following special displays:

Tribute to Geoff Duke.
The museum's collection of sidecar outfits.
Velocette road machines.
Vincent road machines
Sunbeam road machines.
Brough Superior.
Military Machines.
Photo Studio.
Prototypes (x22 machines).
Working Bikes (Police, Ambulance etc)
The Museum's huge collection of BSA & Matchless machines all displayed in numerical/year order.
World Record Breakers (Sprint & Dragsters).
Works Norton Rotaries (All the ex-works Norton Rotary race machines in one place including the famous Steve Hislop 1992 Senior TT winning "White Charger").
1913-14 Matchless V-Twin Works Racer.
Matchless V-Twin Brooklands/TT Works Racer.

There are other special/temporary displays which change on a regular basis.

This is without doubt one of the best motorcycle museums anywhere in the world. It is not just highly recommended, it is a place to dream, to stare, to engage and to re-live memories or make new ones outside on a classic motorcycle. The genius of British motorcycling has a fitting tribute here. Enthralling is perhaps an esoteric word for bikers, yet enthralling is what this place is.

NATIONAL MUSEUM CARDIFF

Cathays Park, Cardiff
CF10 3NP, Cymru.
Tuesday–Sunday, 10am–5pm. Galleries close at 4:45pm.
Phone: 0300 111 2 333
Email: cardiff@museumwales.ac.uk

A collection of transport-related artefacts and some vehicles, notably the oldest surviving Welsh-owned car, a 1900 Benz. Of note, three examples of the Gilbern marque, the only car series produced Wales, are on display.

Exhibits cover tooling, devices, artefacts, memorabilia, tram, bus, and marine subjects. Also of note, the oldest surviving Welsh-built aeroplane, the Robin Goch built around 1908. A small collection of motoring and transport items, well presented in a modern museum, but for the motoring enthusiast of limited attention span.

NATIONAL TRUST CARRIAGE MUSEUM (THE)

Arlington,
Barnstaple, Devon
EX31 4LP. UK.
Opening hours: enquire via National Trust and website.

Often overlooked as it is part of a larger National Trust property, this small museum collection is home to over forty horse-drawn devices – including carts, traps, gigs, coaches, and State carriages. Housed in the Regency property's old stable block there lies a significant collection of carriages dating back over 200 years. A recent exhibit is the Speaker's Coach on loan from the House of Commons. Queen Victoria's pony-hauled Phaeton is also here.

NORTHWEST MUSEUM OF ROAD TRANSPORT

The Old Bus Depot,
Hall Street,
St Helens, WA10 1DU, UK.
Telephone: 01744 451 681
Opening hours: 1000-1500 Saturdays and Sundays only February-December. See website for events dates.
www.nwmort.co.uk

Buses, trams, police cars, classic cars and more are all here in traditional, old bus depot setting and museum context. Formerly the St Helens Transport Museum (1986), this collection is housed in a newly refurbished yet historic bus depot building and is expanding and has restored, running vehicles on offer at the height of the classic vehicle summer season. Annual classic car shows and club gatherings also take place here.

Commercial vehicles/ buses include: Bristol, Crossley, Daimler, Dennis, Leyland, Morris, Dennis, and AEC.

If you are a bus or tram fan, this is also another fine museum within the Liverpool area. The 1890s bus depot makes an evocative setting (amid a refurbished exterior) and Ford fans might care to inspect the police-spec and liveried Escort RS2000 patrol car (registration XEM 650W)! Rarer than you can imagine. The museum is family friendly, although bus and tram fanatics might wish it was just for them.

NORTH YORKSHIRE MOTOR MUSEUM (MATTHEWSONS)

Roxby Garage,
Pickering Road,
Thornton Le-Dale,
North Yorkshire.
YO18 7LH, UK.
Telephone 01751 474455
enquire@matthewsons.co.uk

Monday-Friday 0930-1630. Open weekends to 1600. Note auction day limitations. Telephone in advance for specific museum visit arrangements and remember that auction days are busy and the museum closes to allow stock movements.

A family-run museum and auction house of true grit and real authenticity. They are members of the FBVHC, host many clubs and gatherings, including the all-Party Parliamentary Historic Vehicle Group. Packed with old cars, motorcycles, memorabilia, and offering proper tea. Regular auctions of classic vehicles occur on site and up the road at the village hall.

Founded in 1970, a more recent move to larger premises has allowed the creation of a working garage and museum that is now also the star of *Bangers and Cash,* a recent classic-car-themed television series. The museum has over 40 cars and 30 motorcycles on regular display and a restoration area. Focuses on cars – vintage to modern classic era, and not exclusively British.

Small, easily viewed in an hour or so, with a fee to get in that is less than the cost of a newspaper, this is true, local enthusiasm and run by a great family team of old car fanatics. Fun and full of nostalgia as a small yet very alive motoring 'hub', this is definitely not to be missed for the classic enthusiast. The town and surrounding area are also stunning and an ideal holiday or touring location.

OAKHAM TREASURES TRACTOR & FARM MUSEUM (BRISTOL)

Oakham Treasures, Oakham Farm,
Portbury Lane, Portbury,
Bristol BS20 7SP, UK.
Telephone 01275 375 236
Opening hours: 1000-1700 Tuesday-Saturday
Closed on Sundays, Mondays and Bank Holidays

A tractor and farm implement focus rather than classic cars, but fascinating nonetheless. Oakham (near Bristol, not Oakham, Rutland), houses around 150 old and vintage tractors. Examples can be found from around the world and as far away as America and Australia, from Allis Chalmers to Massey Ferguson and Titan, dating back to a 1918 Fordson.

There's also an impressive display of old farm engines, and there are many examples of both oil and gas fired engines dating back to 1910.

Oakham Treasures is the personal expression of one man's passion for collecting memorabilia. The founder, Keith Sherrell, is a fifth generation West Country Farmer, and began collecting farm machinery in the 1960s as a side-line to his business of buying and selling used farm machinery. Recommended and very atmospheric. Another example of our wonderful museum culture in a differing guise.

ON YOUR MARQUES

Thrumber Marsh lane,
Mumby,
Alford, Lincolnshire,
LN13 9TL, UK.
Telephone: 01507 490 066
www.on-your-marques.co.uk

Not a full motoring museum in the accepted sense, but one worth including because it is a model car museum. This is packed full of model cars that will be familiar to several generations. Highlights include slot cars, models exhibited collectors' plastic cases and a Scalextric track. Small, niche, but committed to the cause nonetheless.

OXFORD BUS MUSEUM AND MORRIS MOTORS MUSEUM

Rail Station,
Long Hanborough,
Oxfordshire.
OX29 8LA, UK.
Telephone: 01993 883 617
Opening hours: 1030-1630 Wednesdays & Sundays. Also Saturdays in June, July, August.
www.Oxfordbusmuseum.org.

Another busman's gem, this time supplemented with the Morris Motors collection which tells the story of William Morris and his motoring empire which was based in Oxford. Mr Morris started the first bus service in Oxford in 1913, *before* he became a global motor magnate. A fine collection of Morris cars and commercials (most Cowley built), are based at this museum.

Over 130 years of bus and transport history is told here – with a local angle. 45 vintage bicycles, cars, and motorcycles are also held. The museum is over 50 years old and runs as a charity. The museums first vehicle was a 1949 AEC Regal III with Willowbrook coachbuilt bodywork. The museum was the first road transport museum to receive a Queens Award for Voluntary Service, in 2018.

Key exhibits include;

AEC (17 examples)
Bedford (OB)
Bristol (VRT)
Daimler (Y-Type of 1915 and Fleetline)
Dennis (Dart and Loline)
Ford (R1040)
Leyland (Atlantean and Leopard)
Morris (FF)

Numerous examples of coachwork are on show. Photographic archive and memorabilia sections are of note. The cafe is good, the access to the buses and cars excellent and the staff very knowledgeable. Enthusiast and family visitors should not be disappointed, although note that 'digital' interface museum culture and interactive 'game' stuff for teenagers are (thankfully) not included. Fascinating.

PALLOT STEAM, MOTOR & GENERAL MUSEUM (THE)

Rue de Bechet,
Trinity,
Jersey,
Channel Islands.
JE3 5BE. UK.
Telephone: 01534 865307
Opening hours: 1000-1700. Monday-Saturday April-October. Winter by appointment.

Named after its founder, Lyndon 'Don' Pallot a well-known Jerseyman, this is like many personal collections, 'different' and all the more compelling and authentic for it. It is a niche offering, but one packed with vital examples of transport and island history. Not quite as old as the Jersey Transport Museum that was established in 1973, Pallot's is nevertheless, a quintessential treasure trove of a personal collection untouched by the fashion for digital re-modelling.

Don Pallot was born in the parish of Trinity in Jersey. He developed an interest in mechanics from an early age and, after leaving school at the age of 14, started remaking bicycles until he became a trainee engineer at Jersey Railways where his enthusiasm for steam was born.

In the early 1930s, Don opened Central Motor Works at Sion, Trinity; this agricultural works was to become well known throughout the island. Pallot was a brilliant engineer who loved solving mechanical problems and his ingenuity led him to invent several implements which were to make the life of the island's farmers easier.

A man of great vision, Don started collecting what he could of mechanical heritage, with his ambition being realised in 1990 with the opening of the Pallot Steam Museum. There is no doubt that without his interest, maintained over many years, much that is on view today would have been lost forever. Locomotives were brought in from the British mainland, Belgium, and Alderney and lovingly restored to form part of his vast and varied collection. Don passed away at the age of 85, but his memory lives on in his Museum which his family continue to operate.

From the Aveling & Porter Steam Roller No: 7807 RR Type, steam locomotives and engines, to cars, motorcycles, bicycles, tractors and agricultural machines, toys, commercials and memorabilia, Pallot's is a time-warp of treasures for those minded to their variety and contexts. If you are on Jersey and are an enthusiast, this is worth the detour.

PATRICK COLLECTION (THE)

Lifford Lane, Kings Norton,
Birmingham, B30 3DY.UK
Telephone: 0121 459 4656
Telephone to check availability

The Patrick Collection is long established and well known to a specific tranche of classic car enthusiasts as a private collection. Note that it is now is visitable by appointment only. The Collection began back in 1960 when a decaying Austin Ten was spotted in a driveway in Hockley Heath. This was no ordinary car however; it had been built by coachbuilders at Patrick Motors Ltd in the 1930s and, after it was purchased for the princely sum of £5, the two men who had originally built it, lovingly restored it to its former glory. Joseph Patrick, chairman of Patrick Motors (garage chain and BL dealerships), was the founding figure of the collection. 240 cars were in the collection, and although sold off via Bonhams, and now reduced in size, loans of cars continue to external bodies continue as does a collection ethos. Patrick's grandson, now works with the collection's small team to preserve the cars and to expand the outreach programme to local schools in a design and technology remit.

The Patrick Collection is owned by the Patrick Foundation, a charitable trust, and contains classic cars and more recent modern classics, notably of up-market marques. There is also a collection of memorabilia including an original Tardis from BBC's *Dr Who* TV series. The Collection is now in a partnership with the Black Country Living Museum.

RIVERSIDE MUSEUM OF TRANSPORT (GLASGOW)

100 Pointhouse Place,
Glasgow, G3 8RS. Scotland.
Telephone: 0141 267 2720
Opening hours: Daily 1000-1700
museums@glasgowlife.org.uk

With over 3,000 exhibits covering, cars, motorbikes and ships, and set on a redeveloped harbour side, this museum was the 2013 European Museum of the Year, and deservedly so. Over 1.2 million visitors per annum now visit what is a jewel in the UK museum movement's crown. Redeveloped using £74 million of grants and amid a charitable trust raising millions, the stunning Zaha Hadid

architecture makes its mark and adds to the experience. The museum has patrons that include: BAE, Rolls-Royce, The Weir group, Strathyclyde Partnership, Arnold Clark, SSE, and the vital Caledonian MacBride. Static and themed exhibits includes buses, trams, cars, bikes, ships and shipbuilding, engineering, railways works and rolling stock and an homage to the Hillman Imp.

Like the Science Museum, Riverside had decide to stack a series of cars in vertical piles on a wall as a 'Wall of Cars'. This looks imposing but renders the cars separate from the viewer and untouchable in every respect. The museum makes reference to the variety of Scottish car marques established over the years – over 40 individual makes – nd of course tributes the clever and rather interesting engineering of Linwood's Scottish-built rear-engined Hillman Imp device.

Exhibits include:

Scottish Cars:
Albion Dog-cart
Albion A3 Tourer
Arrol-Johnson Dog-cart
Arrol-Johnson 1920 Coupe1923 Tourer
Argyll 1900, 1910 & 1913
Galloway Coupe 1924
Other Cars:
1898- 1905 Veteran types
Bentley 4½ Litre
British economy cars (Austin A30, Morris Minor, Ford popular, Berkley
    3-Wheeler, Triumph Mayflower, Standard 10, etc)
Citroen 2CV
BMW Isetta
Messerschmitt micro car,
Hillman Imp display.
Buses
Trams
Motorcycles
Locomotives
Motoring memorabilia
Maritime memorabilia
Shipping collection

This highly recommended museum is surely a 'premier' museum experience and a true example of the 'constructive museum'. One of Scotland's (and Great Britain's) finest museums and known the world over.

ROYAL ELECTRICAL AND MECHANICAL ENGINEERS (REME) MUSEUM

Prince Philip Barracks,
MoD Lyneham,
Calne Road, Lyneham,
Nr Chippenham, Wiltshire.
SN15 4XX, UK.
SN15 4PZ (Sat Nav)
Opening hours: 1000-1630. Tuesday-Saturday
Telephone: 01249 894 869
www.rememuseum.org.uk

Now of official 'Hidden Gem' status from Visit England, the newly re-located REME Museum unites the former REME Aborfield museum and REME Borden store into a larger-scale setting at the former Royal Air Force Lyneham airfield that the RAF Hercules fleet have vacated. Roger Jones MBE and a couple of compatriots started the REME Technology collection while still serving in the Army. The idea was to save historic military vehicles. The task went so well that it became an official Army project and Roger retired from the Army only to then be employed to manage the collection's vehicles at Borden. Twenty-one military vehicles were on public display at the old museum in Aborfield but 85 were in-store at the Bordon reserve collection.

Of note, enthusiasts should note that the REME Museum re-opened in 2017 at its new Wiltshire site equidistant between Swindon and Chippenham.

A collection since 1958, the new museum site provides more space as well as home to the former REME Schools. Of note, REME was formed in 1942 and immediately tested at El Alamein (October 1942) which was the REME's first major combat outing and despite the conditions, the engineers recovered over 1,500 military vehicles including 1,200 tanks. Trades, armour, mechanical and electrical engineering are all part of the REME story – as is the role of women in REME service.

The new site has three main halls and seven galleries. Exhibits include a 1930s Morris pick-up recovery vehicle, an armoured Sherman Beach recovery vehicle and the Bedford mobile machinery truck mobile mechanics repair station while other displays cover the women of REME, a small collection of motorcycles, modified wheeled and tracked and half-tracked vehicles, Scammell Pioneer x4 wheel truck and 1960s-1970s heyday vehicles from ex-colonial operations. There are smaller rooms and galleries with armour and engineering related pieces trades and skills

to study. Of note is a tribute to Major Ivan Hirst and the 1945 VW 'beetle' story with Colonel McEvoy.

Lead exhibits include:

Chieftain 900,
Conqueror
Sherman
BARV
BedfordshireBSAM20
Churchill
Commer Q4
CCRAV
Samson
Matchless G3
Morris Commercial Breakdown
Scammell

A special-interest museum but a very interesting and very good one. Recommended.

SAMMY MILLER MUSEUM

Bashley Cross Roads,
New Milton,
Hampshire, UK.
Telephone: 01425 62077
Opening hours: 1000-1600. Summer, open daily. Note Winter hours/days.
www.sammymiller.co.uk

Another specifically themed British museum and one definitely not to be overlooked, the S.H 'Sammy' Miller Museum was founded and developed by champion ex-racer Sammy Miller MBE and is one of the vital British motorcycling museums. In fact we might suggest it is, in its context, unique and globally famous – it is that good. Miller began his collection when he stored some of his old machines when he set up a motorcycle business in the New Forest in 1964, and the rest really is history. An extension to the museum is planned to further house the growing collection of the man who started out on a 1929 Francis Barnett.

Sammy Miller – 11 times British Trials Champion and European Trials Championship victor, winner of over 1,000 events (road racing and trials) – is clearly a man who knows what is what and is on hand to be consulted. His career

was wide-ranging, he was involved in the Bultaco trials bike story, there were times with Ariel, Honda, on an NSU, and with his500c Ariel HT5 all add to the man's knowledge. Today in his eighties, his enthusiasm belies his age.

Nearly every machine here works and can be ridden and there may be over 400 of them, who knows, he keeps getting more in – a 1938 Zundapp arrived recently. Of notable interest, Miller has rescued the Tait V3 from the late motorcycle designer Bob Tait and built up his final design – the intriguing V3-engined machine, which is on show. The restoration shop is viewable through a large viewing window; shame you can't smell it!

Founded in 1964 and located on the edge of the New Forest in New Milton, Hampshire, it is focused on British and European classics and racers – containing some of the most important racing motorcycles of all time, along with a strong inventory of road going machines. A modern facility that has 'grown up' to become a true bikers shrine.

A nice touch is that many of the motorcycles are mounted on plinths to waist height which makes appreciating them much easier. Sammy's ex-works 1957 250cc DOHC Mondial of world championship contention is on show.

Packed full of motorcycles of various types, including one-offs and prototypes, (including the Moto Guzzi V8) and a 1950 Bicilindrical, a recent acquisition is the 1964 Grand Prix Bianchi. Also a new arrival is the 1939 BSA Empire Gold Star. There is also much motorcycling memorabilia. The museum includes a Norton hall, Trials Bike Hall, a Racing Hall. Sports, and road bikes also get their own halls. Vincent and flat tank machines also have their own room. Exotic bikes, engines and much more make up one of the largest and best motorcycle collections in the world. The museum's Sammy Miller, Bob Stanley and John Ring are all available for conversation.

The museum's 'bike jumble' is a niche alternative to Beaulieu's autojumble (sorry Beaulieu).

The on-site Bashley Manor Tea rooms serve homemade cake and proper tea but can be busy – because the cake is so good. There is plenty of room for children to remain well-behaved too.

This place is utterly engaging and a true enthusiasts' shrine of global renown yet also family friendly. Highly recommended and of course it's a biker's 'bucket list' necessity. There are hours of fun and interest to be had here. Try to chat with Sammy if he is about.

Since when were private collections or trusts this good? The answer, is that this is now the standard to expect. This place is a significant achievement and you cannot miss it, even if you are not a full-on motorcyclist, car and 'mechanical' people will be enthralled for sure and Beaulieu is just down the road; just do not try to both museums in the same day unless forced to by circumstance as you will do neither justice.

SCALEBY HILL VINTAGE MOTORCYCLE MUSEUM/MIKE BARRY MUSEUM

The Cottage,
Chappel Lane,
Carlisle,
CA6 4LY, UK.
Telephone: 01228 675 117.

Unadvertised, not obvious internationally (yet globally famous amongst those in the know), run by one man (Mike Barry), and definitely niche, this small motorcycle museum also happens to be authentic and one of the best, most engaging small museums in Great Britain. That the proprietor is knowledgeable and a true enthusiast, is the icing on the cake. He is a dog man too, which makes him even more acceptable. A cuppa and slice of homemade cake seem suddenly vital.

The oldest machine in the collection is a 1926 Douglas, while, MV Augusta, Gilera, Honda, Ducati, Triumph, BSA Excelsior, Coventry Eagle, Francis Barnet, Velocette, Douglas, also feature as does the owner's own BSA racing sidecar outfit.

Mike Barry, a former racing champion, began restoring bikes while recuperating from a serious crash. His recovery has been to amass and restore a collection of over 50 motorcycles amid a hall of memorabilia and artefacts of a sporting life.

As well as motorcycles, exhibits include games machines, models, large-scale radio-controlled aeroplanes and railway and motoring memorabilia; there are also a classic Jaguar saloon and an Austin van, both of which are in regular road use. Many of the motorcycles which date from the 1920s up to the late 1960s are road legal. Sidecars also feature.

It might be a long way from the London bubble, but for the true enthusiast, this small museum does more than tick boxes. The man should be given a medal. For motorcyclists, it is said that this is a 'must see' job.

SCIENCE MUSEUM (THE)

Science Museum,
Exhibition Road, South Kensington,
London, SW7 2DD, UK.
Open daily: 1000–1800

A national resource of vital importance, the Science Museum does in fact offer only a limited view of British automotive engineering and motoring history.

The space devoted to cars is small and the museums wider emphasis seems to be on interactive displays and digital engagement for youth. Cars stacked up on a wall looked great but prevents actual touching or study of their forms.

The transport section is good, covering cars, aircraft, rail, and shipping, but recent fashions have seen changes to the museum's displays and techniques that some may question – others may not.

The problem lies in space, and an old building amid differing visitor needs and marketing thinking. But the issue may also lie in the decision taken for displays. Yet the Science Museum rarely opens its wonderful store at Wroughton in Wiltshire where its true motoring and mechanical treasures are stored. Therein lie significant and rare automotive and aviation items of global importance, yet little is seen of them. The archive library (by appointment) is also based at Wroughton.

The London Science Museum is of course worth a visit, but the motoring section seems lacking something.

Exhibits include:

Ariel quadri-cycle, 1900.
Austin Seven prototype, 1922.
B.S.A. 10 H.P. Scout motor cycle engine and front wheel drive transmission unit, 1936.
Bond Minicar with 122 c.c.,1950
Citroen type DS19 automatically guided motor car.
Connaught Grand Prix racing car, 1955, powered by an Alta 2 1/2 litre straight four engine
Daimler, Kimberley model, 4.1/2 hp motor car, 1901,
Daimler-Maybach motor car, 1895.
DAF 'Daffodil' car, 1965
Darracq car, 1898.
D.K.W. Sonderklasse 896 c.c, 1959.
E.R.A. motor car, 1937, scale model.
Ford Zephyr car chassis, 1956, sectioned.
Gardner-Serpollet steam car, 1903.
G.N. Cyclecar, 1921.
Humberette car, 1903.
Humber Snipe, 1961
Lagonda saloon car, 1957.
Napier '40/50' limousine motor car, 1921.
N.S.U. Spider with Wankel rotary engine, 1965.
Perkins 4 cylinder compression-ignition motor car diesel engine with electric motor, 1963.
Petrol-electric car, based on Fiat 8 H.P. open two-seater, 1927.

Rolls-Royce Silver Cloud Mark I car chassis, 1955
Rover gas turbine motor car, JET
'White' Steam Motor Car, 10HP, Period 1903-1905

The Science Museum's main store is located at:

SCIENCE MUSEUM WROUGHTON

Red Barn Gate, Wroughton, Swindon, Wiltshire.
Contact information
Telephone: 01793 846200
Closed to the public except on open days and via organised tours. Library and archive open by appointment only.

Aircraft, cars, steam engines, static engines, commercials, tractors and buses are all stored at Wroughton. Over 100 cars and motorcycles are stored. The archives are incredibly diverse and have over 10,000 documents.

There are ten hangars housing over 30,000 items. Rarities include the world's first 'driverless' or autonomous self-steering car in the form of the 1959 Citroen DS self-steering, solid-state electrics-guided prototype. A hydrogen fuel-cell powered DAF made by Shell in 1967 underlines the historical facts – as do pre-1900 vehicles including a Stankey steam car.

Rare aircraft include:

de Havilland Comet 4
de Havilland / Hawker Siddely Trident 1, and 3b.
Douglas DC3
Ford Edsel
Boeing 247
Handley Page Gugnunc
Lockheed Constellation (ex-KLM and Rolling Stones!)

If you can get in, (and I have) this is treasure beyond imagining. Superbly run, and with such rare content, somehow, this needs opening up and made to pay its way. Air shows and open days used to be held here. Television car programmes are regular visitors to this airfield that once repaired RAF bombers. Lobbying the Science Museum or your MP might help get this place opened up – after all, don't we the people 'own' it and its contents?

Note – The Science Museum Group also includes the Science and Industry Museum, Liverpool Road, Manchester M3 4FP, UK.

SCOTTISH VINTAGE BUS MUSEUM (THE)

M90 Commerce Park,
Lathalmond by Dunfermline,
Fife, KY12 0SJ. Scotland.
Opening hours: Sundays, April-October
www.svbm.online

With over 160 buses from the 1920s to the 1990s, this really is a major bus museum and a significant stop-off for bus enthusiasts from all over the world. Thirty other road vehicles including commercials and cars are also held. The Exhibition Hall houses vehicles and artefacts as well as the museum cafe and shop.

The late 1970s and early 1980s had seen a build-up of vehicles for preservation in Scotland and these were stored in farms, bus depots, etc. An initial approach to preservationists about a combined storage/museum set-up was met with a favourable response; until then they had been working in small groups or on their own and the hunt was on for suitable premises. From such a basis emerged this excellent transport museum that brought all the diverse strands of machines and storage together under one roof. Several locations have been used since the mid-1980s and the collection is now at a permanent site. The SVBM is run on a purely voluntary basis.

Key highlights include buses from Scotland, England, Northern Ireland, Hong Kong and Australia. Special bodies and chassis and of interest, Weymann, Park Ward, and Mulliner, bodies feature alongside the usual coachwork providers. The oldest bus here is the 1928 Leyland Titan. A 1928 Leyland Titan, and a 1929 Leyland Tiger provide continuity to the start of the collection. There are some very nice Albions, Bristols, and AECs dating from the 1950s to the1970s.

This is a really serious bus museum for the bus enthusiast, and it is interesting for the general transport enthusiast as well. Significant historical bus-related content can be found in this great place.

SHUTTLEWORTH COLLECTION (THE)

Old Warden Aerodrome,
Hill Lane, Biggleswade,
Bedfordshire, SG18 9EP, UK.
Telephone: 01767 627927
www.shuttleworth.org
Opening times: Summer, 7 days a week 0930-1700. Winter, 1000-1600.
Fly-in to runway by prior arrangement and rating. Radio frequency is 130.705

This, is nostalgia on steroids and essential visiting. The Shuttleworth Collection (operating as a Trust) was created in 1940 by Dorothy Shuttleworth as a tribute to the life of her son Richard Ormonde Shuttleworth, a 1930s car and aircraft enthusiast who was killed in the Second World War aged just thirty-one.

Shuttleworth owned and piloted his own a superb de Havilland aircraft and raced an Alfa Romeo P3 Tipo B chassis no. 5007 in the world Grand Prix championship. He won the 1935 Donington Grand Prix in the Alfa and, was a regular in the London-Brighton run, where today his cars still compete. A green Bugatti T51, a Railton, and Rolls-Royces all passed through his ownership. A sleeve-valved Sparkbrook motorcycle was at one time Richard's personal steed. His Bleriot XI and his Deperdussin monoplane formed the basis of his early collection.

Not only is this an indoor venue, but it offers wonderful live outdoor events, air shows on its own runway, car shows, and 'sunset' events of sublime significance. If you love old aircraft, cars, motorcycles, and wheeled devices that are kept in working order and displayed at work, this is the place to feed that passion. Photographic opportunities abound at the Shuttleworth collection. Vintage buses also operate on site. The cafe offers a high quality experience and the Old Warden mansion house and garden also offer a family experience.

Static displays and live flying days amid many themed vehicle displays and tributes allow the collection to provide memorable and significant to visitors. Shuttleworth also holds a 'Bikers' Special' event. Through such efforts and wider collaborations, Shuttleworth now occupies a vital position on the national and international scene. It is also offers a research and educational remit. The house and Swiss garden also offer further interest amid the legacy of the Shuttleworth family.

Opened to the public in 1963, with further aircraft and vehicles added over the years, the Shuttleworth Collection is a registered charity, self-funded through daily admission and ticket sales. A Shuttleworth College opened in 1946 focuses on agrarian matters and reflects the Shuttleworth family's agricultural engineering history under the company of Clayton and Shuttleworth.

Recently somewhat aped by live and re-enactment events at Brooklands, it was the Shuttleworth Collection which innovated 'live' outdoor events and gatherings where ancient aircraft and vehicles can be seen up close in action, as intended by their creators.

Key exhibits include:

Vintage aircraft: 1909-1950s
Veteran Vehicles, Edwardian cars, early dogcarts, commercials including buses, and 1930s-1940s cars. Key vehicles include:

1896 Benz Dogcart
1898 Panhard-Levassor

1900 Marot Gardan
1901 Arrol-Johnstone

1899 Mors
1901 Locomobile
1901 Stanley Steamer
1902 Peugeot
1902 American Buddy
1903 de Dietrich Type SM
1903 Richard Brasier
1912 Crossley T5
1912 Wolsely M5
1912 Ford Model T Tourer,
1913 McCurd 5 Ton Lorry
1913 Morris Oxford
1913 Wellingborough

1920 Hucks Starter
1920 Rickshaw
1921 Charabus
1924 Leyland White Rose
1924 Bean
1926 Jowett Type C
1931 Austin Burnham
1934 Austin Seven AAK
1937 Fiat Topolino
1937 Railton
1938 Hillman Minx
1939 MG Midget
1943 Fordson WOT 2H

Classic Motorcycles:

1904 Aurora
1900 Single Motor Wheel
1919 Stafford Pup
1920 ABC
1921 Scott Squirrel
1924 Triumph Type SD
1929 Ariel Model A
1940 BSA M20
1948 BSA Bantam

1948 Norton Big 4
1950 Sunbeam SB
1952 Brackhouse Corgi
1955 BSA A7
1958 New Hudson
1948 Phillips Cyclemsater
1962 Norton Model ES2
   Combi
1967 Raleigh Wing

Veteran bicycles include a penny farthings and a boneshaker.
   Agricultural exhibits include a team engine, working chaff cutter, living van and tractors
   Engineering Workshop:

Hangar 1: First World War
Hangar 2: Second World War
Hangar 3: Clayton & Shuttleworth
Hangar 4: Leading Edge
Hangar 5: Transport Pioneers
Hangar 6: Flying High

The Shuttleworth Collection operates an online library ('Bleriot') as a free service and an archival catalogue. The online catalogue is a major addition to the Archive Research Service. It contains in excess of 10,000 records of books, letters and photographic material and is an on-going project and can be contacted via library@shuttleworth.org

For the one-make enthusiast, and for those with a wider marque interest across winged and wheeled mechanical machines in a historical context, Shuttleworth (collection, house and Swiss garden) provides a truly authentic, classless, yet exquisite experience that is of international significance. Richard Shuttleworth's personality and ethos surely lives on through this place – one that is definitely not to be missed. Highly recommended and a very British day out. Memories are made of this.

SOUTH YORKSHIRE TRANSPORT MUSEUM

9 Waddington Way, Aldwarke,
Rotherham, S65 3SH, UK.
Open on the second Sunday each month from 1030-1600. See website for special dates and events.
www.sytm.co.uk

The South Yorkshire Transport Museum (formerly the Sheffield Bus Museum) does 'what it says on the tin' and is a transport (bus) related non-profit organisation which relies on donations, sponsorship, funding and the help of its volunteers to keep it running.

Featuring 10 buses, several commercials, a tram, and classic cars and vans, amid a collection of memorabilia, this is a Yorkshire-focused transport museum. Workshop tours are conducted upon request where you can view on-going restoration projects. Refreshments are served in the cafe and there are souvenirs and memorabilia on sale. Small, but very authentic this is a bus enthusiasts vital stop-off.

STANFORD HALL (MOTORCYCLE) MUSEUM

Stanford Hall,
Lutterworth,
Leicestershire,
LE17 6DH UK.
Telephone: 01788 860250
Opening hours: 1000-1730 daily. Seasonal variations. See website for events days.
www.stanfordhall.co.uk

A long-established collection of classic, vintage and racing motorcycles. Created under the guidance of the founder of the Vintage Motorcycle Club (VMCC) C.E. Allan and members, it continues to provide a base for VMCC members and events. Over 70 machines are held.

Set amid the grounds of the stately home, this museum offers the motorcycle enthusiast the sight of rare, early-era racing machines, and a venue for numerous motorcycle club events and gatherings.

Exhibits include:

1914 AJS 350
1923-1954 AJS motorcycles
1913 BAT 770cc
1922 Brough Superior, 1000cc JAP-engined
1930 Brough Superior 1000cc and sidecar
1913 BSA 500cc
1914 Douglas 300cc
1953 Gilera 500c
1963 Greeves 250scc 2-stroke
1929 Guzzi 500cc 4-valve
1912 JAP 200cc Special-interest
1907-1961 Norton collection
1963 Beart/Norton 350cc
1958 NSU 250cc
1926 Rex 350cc
1920-1930 Rudge collection
1910-1947 Tirumph collection
1929-1967 Velocette collections
1910 Vindec 8hp

There are also numerous touring motorcycles, three wheelers and memorabilia.

An unusual setting in a stately home for a motoring collection, and thus also family friendly and highly recommended by all for its contents, the staff, and events and special motoring days.

STREETLIFE MUSEUM OF TRANSPORT

Museums Quarter,
Hull,
HU1 1NQ, UK.
Telephone: 01482 613902
Opening hours: 1000-1630 daily

The Streetlife Museum of Transport is a transport museum located in Kingston upon Hull, England. The roots of the collection date back to the early twentieth century, however the purpose-built museum the collection is housed in was opened

in 1989. Core areas of the collection include veteran cars, horse-drawn carriages and objects relating to local public transport.

The museum forms part of the Museums Quarter in Hull, based on the historic High Street in the Old Town of the city. Of note is the Gardner Serpollet steam car 1901 and the AEC buses. An old museum reinterpreted to the new museum age. It might have lost some of its old world charm but has gained much in terms of displays and engagement.

STONEHURST FARM MOTOR MUSEUM

Bond Lane,
Mountsorrel,
Leicestershire, LW12 7AA. UK.
Telephone: 01509 413 216
Opening hours: 0930-1700 daily.
www.stonehurstfarmpark.co.uk

This is the Duffin family collection amassed over several decades and located within a family visitor attraction farm park. Over fifty classic cars and motorcycles and a large collection of automobilia feature and includes an Edwardian bus and a 1911 Ariel motorcycle. Cars include veteran and modern classics.

Packed with petroliana, memorabilia, working cars and motorcycles in a classic 'shed' environment, this is well worth a visit but car enthusiasts must appreciate that it is set amid a family friendly, 'farm-park' set up. Note that entry to the car museum is free, only as part of the general farm park admission price. A small but very good, niche museum.

STUDIO434

434-436 Mutton Lane,
Potters Bar, Hertfordshire EN6 3AT, UK.
Telephone: 01707 642 514
enquiry@studio434.co.uk

Studio 434 is not a museum, but it is a museum quality collection of a vast and varied mix of classic cars of many eras that are the personal catalogue of one man. Although not open to the public, Studio 434 is open by prior agreement to car clubs and interested organisations.

The owner, Rodger Dudding, is a successful entrepreneur ranked in the UK 'rich list' who has amassed a personal collection of over 300 cars and motorcycles.

He has created Studio434 as a car storage facility (550 cars storage), but seems to have stored more than enough of his own cars in a stunning setting. The building also hosts motoring events, filming, and launches. It is effectively a new take on car storage and car collecting as a 'hub' or host.

The Studio434 collection includes: Aston Martins, Bentleys, Clynos Jaguars, Austins, Fords, Land Rovers, Lagondas, Triumphs, several Rovers, a Jensen FF, a Ferrari Dino, a Citoroen DS convertible, a Morris Minor, the AC 378 Zagato Prototype, a BMW Isetta, Maserati Khamsin, Karmann Ghia, and a marvellous collection of motorcycles, memorabilia and automotive artefacts.

If you are an official car club or group or association and want to view a stunning collection that is quietly presented through the philanthropic kindness of just one man, then contact him at Studio434. You will not be disappointed. This place is, to quote modern speech, 'amazing'.

SWANSEA BUS MUSEUM

Unit 2, Viking Way,
Winch Wen Industrial Estate,
Swansea, SA1 7DA. Cymru
Telephone: 01792 732832
Opening hours: Sundays 1100-1600
www.swtpg.org.uk

Swansea Bus Museum restores, operates and displays buses of public transport companies of South and West Wales. The significant collection consists primarily of vehicles from South Wales together with two examples of original London Transport Routemasters. At time of writing, the museum was in the middle of re-location. It offers a major collection of buses across several decades and is a vital part of the bus enthusiasts culture.

An impressive collection mainly consists of vehicles operated by South Wales Transport (SWT) and First Cymru. The museum is also home to a selection of American cars, commercial vehicles and Land Rovers.

Main contents:

Leyland Tiger PS1, GTX 437. Body: Neath Coachworks B33F
AEC Regent V MD3RV, MCY 407. Fleet no. 447. Engine AV470, 7.75 litre. Body MCW Orion H32/28R
RM66
AEC Routemaster VLT 66. LT Fleet number RM66
AEC Routemaster WLT 308. LT Fleet number RM308
AEC Regent V 2D3RA, 11 BWN, Fleet No. 571. Body: Willowbrook H39/32F. Engine AV 590, 9.6-litre

AEC Regent V 2D3RA, 282 DWN, Fleet number 38, Body: Roe B37F

AEC Regent V 154 FCY. Fleet number 586. Body: Willowbrook. Seats: 71. Engine AV 590, 9.6-litre.

AEC Regent V 423 HCY. Fleet number 590. Engine AEC AV691, 11.3L. Body: Weymann H39/32F M1467

AEC Regent V 2D3RA, GWN 867E. Body: 27' Willowbrook. Fleet no. 639. Seats 64

AEC Reliance 6MU3R, KKG 215F. Body: Marshall DP41F. Engine: AV505

Leyland National Mark 1 HLZ 4439 (GCY 748N). Body: East Lancs/Greenway B52F

Leyland National Mark 1, JTH 756P

Bristol VRT, MOD 571P. Chassis: VRT/SL3/1457. Engine: Gardner 6LXB. Body: ECW O43/32F

Bristol LH6L NDE 916 R. Chassis LH-1309. Engine: Leyland O401. Body: Eastern Coachworks B45F

Bristol VR, RTH 931S. Chassis: VRT/SL3/1011. Engine: Leyland O501/ Gardner 6LX. Body: Eastern Coachworks CO43/31F

Bristol VRT WTH 961T. Chassis: VRT/SL3/1855. Engine: Gardner 6LXB. Body: ECW H43/31F

AEC Reliance 760, BTH 365V. Body: Duple Dominant II

Bristol VRT, BEP 978V. Chassis: VRT/SL3/2299. Engine: Leyland O501 Body: ECW H43/31F

Leyland Tiger, NTH 263X. Body: Plaxton Viewmaster Express

Leyland Olympian, C903 FCY. Body: Eastern Coachworks H45/30F

Mercedes Benz L608D, D230 LCY. Body: Robin Hood B20F

Dennis Dart 9SDL, L501 HCY. Body: Plaxton Pointer B35F

Dennis Dart SFD, P137 TDL. Body: UVG Urbanstar B43F

Dennis Dart 9.2 SLF, P580 BTH. Body: Plaxton Pointer B31F

Volvo B10M, P339 VWR. Body: Plaxton C53F

Bedford OB, FUT 58. Body: Duple C29

ULSTER TRANSPORT MUSEUM

Cultura,
Holywood,
Belfast, BT180EU, Northern Ireland.
Telephone: 00 44 028 9042 8428
Opening hours: 1000-1700: see website for day details.

There is a rich heritage of car, ship, aircraft, and tractor building and industrial engineering in Belfast – way above the De Lorean fiasco. This museum covers

everything from trams and buses to the Crosslé racing car, and the interesting life of Rex McCandless and his version of a 'Jeep' type 4x4 in the post-war years.

Strong local displays and a range of cars add to the mix.

The car gallery features a display of De Lorean cars alongside, Peugeot, MG, Mercedes, Morris, Riley, Hillman and Ford. There is also a small vintage garage

Of note is the Crosslé display. John Crosslé designed and built the Crosslé Mk3 and raced it at Kirkistown, Phoenix Park and Dunboyne race tracks. The Crosslé Car Company was founded in 1959 when this car was built, and the firm continues to build and repair racing cars in Holywood, County Down.

The McCandless Mule was a 'Go Anywhere' concept vehicle from the early 1950s. The four-wheel-drive Mule combined light weight with low cost construction and ease of maintenance. It was designed by local inventor Rex McCandless..

So, a McCandless Manx Norton Motorcycle 1952 frames the Rex McCandless story. He was a successful motorcycle racer who designed the legendary 'Featherbed' frame. This frame was strong and rigid, making a motorcycle easier to control. Norton adopted the frame for use on its successful racing motorbikes, which dominated the sport in the 1950s.

Isabel Woods' Mercian Racing Bicycle 1953 frames the Isabel Woods (née Clements) display. She was born in 1928. She notched up eight world records while cycling for Belfast Cycling Clubs in the 1950s. Most famously, she held the Ladies 'end-to-end' Irish cycling record – from Mizen Head in Cork to Fair Head, near Ballycastle – from June 1955 to July 2007. Her record-breaking time was 23 hours, 0 minutes and 3 seconds.

The Ulster Transport Museum contains one of the most comprehensive transport collections in Europe including an assortment of vintage motorbikes, horse-drawn carriages and locomotives.

Another excellent regional museum that delivers a superb experience and learning.

WHITEWEBBS MUSEUM OF TRANSPORT

Whitewebbs Lane,
Enfield,
EN2 9HP, UK.
Telephone: 020 8367 1898
Opening hours: 1000-1600 Tuesdays and the last Sunday a month. See website for special events and days
www.whitewebbsmuseum.co.uk

Run by the Enfield and District Veteran Vehicle Trust, and self-funding, this is lovely example of what a small, volunteer-run museum can achieve with funds, commitment and dedication. Several hours are needed to see everything. The entry fee is modest.

Cars, motorcycles, fire engines, commercials and memorabilia are all housed in a Victorian water pumping station. Attractions include: toys, models; model railway; railwayana; a regular autojumble; commercial vehicles; bicycles; enamel sign collection, all of it spread over four floors of the original mill and into a new building. Boasts a great cafe.

Over 40 vintage and classic motorcycles are on show. Modern classics include a lovely Peugeot 304 coupe, early Mk1 Capri, Austins, Jaguar, Ferrari, Lotus; vintage and pre-1939 carts and commercials.

This museum also runs the Enfield Pageant of Motoring. There are regular club visitors including the, Classic Ford Club, Saab Owners Club, and the BSA Club to name just some. American cars gather here too.

With a 'courtyard' setting, relaxed atmosphere and excellent exhibits, it is great for the dedicated enthusiast, but also family friendly. Highly recommended. Give them a gold star!

WILLIAMS F1 MUSEUM/CONFERENCE CENTRE

Williams Engineering Ltd,
Grove,
Wantage, Oxfordshire, OX12 0DQ, UK.
www.williamsf1.com

The stunning and vital Williams F1 historic Grand Prix and heritage collection is housed at the Williams HQ near Oxford and is open at various times throughout the year for pre-booked guided tours. It can also be used via a conference centre for an event booking – by fans, clubs or corporates.

The museum houses the largest private collection of F1 cars; the heritage department houses all aspects of the work of Williams as a team and as a consulting engineering company over the years.

Brilliantly displayed with stunning exhibits and visual interpretations, this is for the Williams fan, or any F1 fan, a shrine that is of the highest quality. Jonathan Williams runs the facility with Mr R. Stanford who has been with Williams for three decades, including as team manager.

The displays cover not just F1 cars, but also the specials and prototypes created by Williams Engineering over many years for car manufacturers. Detailed, engaging, and fascinating from whichever angle you look at it, this is a superb facility and no wonder it is often booked out – F1 fans love it and rightly so. Highly recommended for enthusiasts, but do concentrate!

WIRRAL TRANSPORT MUSEUM & HERITAGE TRAMWAY

1 Taylor Street,
Birkenhead,
Liverpool,
CH41 1BG, UK.
Telephone: 0151 647 2128
Opening Hours: weekdays and other times. See website
If electric trams are your thing, this is the place to go, not least as they work and you can ride on them. Recently revamped, the museum also has cars, motorcycles, buses, transport ephemera and a model railway. Described by many as true hidden gem, this is transport heritage that lives. The trams are wonderfully restored and very cheap to ride on – and museum access is free!

WYTHALL TRANSPORT MUSEUM

Chapel Lane,
Wythall, B47 6JA, UK.
Telephone: 01564 826471
Opening hours: 1100-1600 weekends. Open Wednesdays in school holidays. See website for variances and events
www.wythall.org.uk

A bus and transport hub based south of Birmingham and another gem of busman's authenticity. Originally begun in 1973 as a preservation society group and set up in 1977 by a charity (a Birmingham and Midland Omnibus Trust), the museum is now a significant bus collection and post- 2016, a renamed charity. A large site with covered and insulated storage allows buses to now be restored and kept in wonderful condition. Donations and a heritage lottery grant have modernised the museum in recent years. Buses and battery-electric vehicles are the focus of the collection.

Nearly 100 buses reside here and tell the story of local Midlands bus operations across many decades. The buses are often run and special events days are advertised via the website.

Key exhibits are the Midland Red Collection, West Midlands Collection and other buses and coaches.

The Midland Red collection contains original buses dating from 1913, through the 1920s and beyond to 1976. Clearly, these are significant vehicles to any bus enthusiast.

As well as the bus 'sheds', there are three display halls, each with a theme. Hall 1 shows off buses and bus operations. Hall 2 contains a large collection electric (battery) powered historic vehicles and 30 milk floats! Hall 3 allows the visitor to see working buses in restoration.

Model railways (the Elmdon Model Engineering Society is based here) and memorabilia also feature.

Family-friendly with a safe area for children and a good cafe. If you are into buses, this is one not to be missed. The level of nostalgia and colourful bus designs and liveries would surely appeal to any transport enthusiast. Runs out on the old buses are great fun and the staff know their stuff. Highly recommended.

Author's Personal Pick of Global Museums

Aerospace Bristol, UK
Atwell-Wilson Museum, UK
British Commercial Vehicle Museum, UK
British Motor Museum, UK
Brooklands Museum, UK
Bugatti Trust Museum, UK
Haynes International Museum, UK
Isle of Man Motor Museum/Cunningham Collection, UK
Lakeland Museum, UK
Moray Motor Museum, UK
National Motor Museum, UK
National Motorcycle Museum, UK
Sammy Miller Museum, UK
Shuttleworth Museum, UK
Charlie's Auto Museum, Australia
Château de Savigny-les-Beaune/M. Pont Museum, France
BMW Museum, Germany
Garlits Museum of Drag Racing, USA
Ferrari Museum, Italy
Lohéac/Manoir Automobile Museum, France
Mullin Automotive Museum, America
NSU/Two Wheel Museum, Germany
Porsche Museum, Germany
Saab Museum, Sweden
Qantas Founders Museum, Australia
York Motor Museum, Australia

Above: Thunderbirds are go! American metal speeds away from the Cotswold Vintage Extravaganza.

Left: It's a Citroën – gull wing design seen at the Conservatoire. (Photo: Citroën)

The author at the wheel of the Michael Read private collection 1914 Chater Lea Singer Special with Lionel Martin engine and 'buff form' to match.

Bright blue looks good on old bikes as well as on old cars. Atwell-Wilson Museum, Calne.

Inside the Rolls-Royce Merlin engine. A rare view of the vital internals of the ultimate engineering.

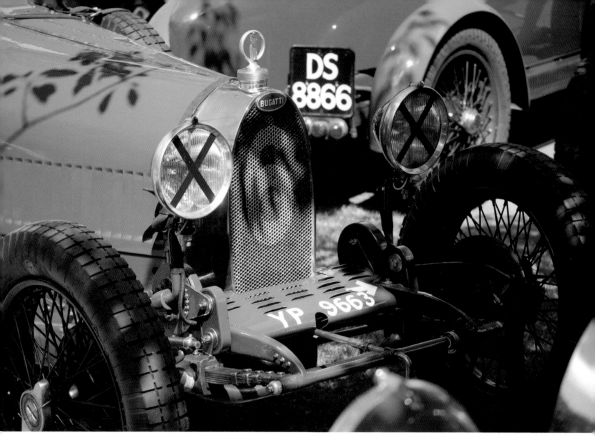

Above: Bugatti heaven. Types 35, 37 and 40 all in blue at Prescott.

Right: Original Fordson metal – true nostalgia.

Above: All the fun of Brooklands – a living museum.

Left: Autojumble exhibits at Beaulieu.

The rare four-door Citroen SM captured in detail.

Best of British? Blackburn Buccaneer and an Allard at Kemble.

A French-built, early GN in the car park at the living museum that is the Goodwood car park.

Mercedes-Benz Woody. Woodies are a rare and wonderful niche in the classic car world.

Citroen SM – designed by Robert Opron and team. French design at its ultimate freedom.

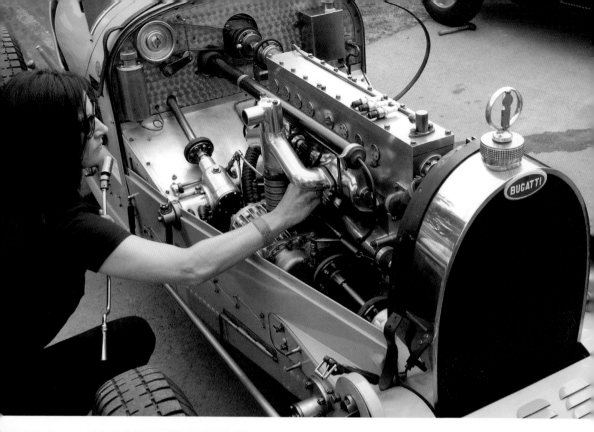

Above: Mrs Gentry of Gentry Restorations attends to the supercharged Type 35 straight-eight at Prescott.

Left: Rust in Peace. French grille artefacts found in deepest France.

Above: Ford GT40 at speed at Goodwood's museum that isn't.

Right: The 'face' of 1960s Aston Martin, truly classic.

Boat-tailed beauty at Bicester. Another living museum day at Bicester. OSV 136, the 1935 Austin Seven Ulster.

BEYOND BRITAIN

Notes on selected non-UK museums & global listing

Below can be found selected out-takes describing museums beyond Great Britain, and there follows a comprehensive listing of the leading, national car museums across the world. Full details can be accessed from the museums respective websites.

AUSTRALIA

CHARLIE'S AUTO MUSEUM

147 Purves Road,
Arthur's Seat, VIC.
Telephone: 0419 887 801

Here lie two 'sheds' on a headland surrounded by calm bays on the Mornington Peninusla – classic car and motorcycle country and en-route to the stunning Great Ocean Road and its superb driving, bends, and cafes at Apollo Bay and beyond.

At Charlie's, there are more than fifty cars and motorcycles with memorabilia and models, Charles Schwerkolt the owner is a real character and true petrol-head. He has spent decades collecting cars and memorabilia. He has a racing pedigree too. He has also created his own cafe restaurant and a huge following.

A collector for 25 years, Charlie has Studebakers as his favoured marque, yet there is even a Tatra here, and Reliant Robins. There are also Maseratis, Porsche, Jeep, Trabant, MG TD, and much more, including big Aussie V8 stuff.

This is true, 'shed' paradise and also pure Aussie style in a relaxed and easy manner. You cannot miss it if you like cars and motorcycles. The cafe is great too.

NATIONAL MOTORCYCLE MUSEUM

33 Clarkson Street,
Nabiac, Nr Newcastle, New South Wales 2312,
Opening Hours: 0900-1600 daily

800, yes 800 motorcycles collected in a series of very Australian barns or sheds, this is the dedicated work of the Kelleher family over many years. Unofficially, the 'national' Motorcycle museum. Some machines are on loan, others owned by the museum. A lot of them run.

Hot, a bit dusty (what would you expect out here?) and not as 'pretty' as some architectural museum delights aspire too, this is a great place. Its rammed with the history of Aussie-rules motorcycling from city to rural farm and beyond. There are motorcycles here that even experts will have never seen. Truly a shrine to all thing two-wheeled in an Aussie vein. Definitely recommended, but just don't expect 'new age of the museum' digital delight.

PANORAMA MOTORCYCLE MUSEUM

3 Panorama Drive, Roadvale, Queensland,
Opening hours: Sundays 0800-1600 and by appointment

Not to be confused with Mount Panorama, this family run gem is a stunning private collection that tributes its founder Rod Jurgensen. As such it is not a for-profit operation, but that does not stop it being brilliant for bikers. Now run by Rod's family, this is not just a static park of interesting machines, it is a warm and enthusiastic tribute to decades of collecting and fettling. Originally a museum collection run by Rod in the 1970s, it has now been relaunched and is growing.

Motorcycles, cars, militaria, memorabilia and more are here. AJS, Ariel, BA, Harley-Davidson, Indian, Triumph, Matchless and more are all on show. A 1914 Indian is the oldest machine present and a 1942 Indian Chief and side car is the most valuable, says the museum.

This museum is a typical Australian private affair of huge dedication and of course, is in a large 'shed'. Again, don't expect digital, just sup at the grail of much-loved machines.

THE POWERHOUSE MOTORCYCLE MUSEUM

250 Armidale Road, New England Highway, Tamworth, NSW 2340.
Opening hours: 0900-1700 daily

Cleverly located as part of a hotel, this small but shiny museum, contains just over fifty interesting motorcycles in working order and mainly dating

from the 1950s-1970s. All have been restored. BSA, Ducati, Triumph, Honda, Norton, Velocette, Laverda, and a rare MV Augusta F4 ORO series.

Although 'roped off', the collection is of note and worth a couple of hours of your time. Complimentary tea and refreshments served.

These three smaller motorcycle museums may not be the biggest or perhaps even the 'best' on a global basis but they are stars of the private collection firmament and the Australian 'authentic' museum movement. There is real enthusiasm and dedication here in this Australian sub-culture of the smaller museum and collection. An equally interesting and committed private collection, albeit a touch more upmarket is the Robert Stein collection. Stein's vintage motorcycle collection and winery at Mudgee, New South Wales is eclectic, smart, and well worth a visit. But if you are on a motorcycle, where will you put the wine you buy?

YORK MOTOR MUSEUM

116 Avon Terrace,
York. W.A. 6302
Telephone; 0061 8 96411288
Opening hours: 0900-1600 daily
www.yorkmotormuseum.com

Hidden away behind old colonial era architecture in a hot town on the edge of the Western Australian farm lands that lead further to the outback of beyond, York is that rare thing, a community museum that is off the beaten track yet which contains important exhibits. It can be a hot and dusty drive from Perth, but it is well worth the visit. I recommended the museum to *Classic and Sports Car* magazine, whose man was not disappointed when he got there.

Now operated by the Avon Valley Museum Association, yet originally inspired by the collection of WA Motoring enthusiast Peter Briggs, York makes the most of the often-forgotten history of Australian rural motoring and motorsport. This is a community-run museum as opposed to solely being a commercial business.

Some of the exhibits were previously seen in the now closed Fremantle Docks Museum – notably an early 1950s Saab. The museum does of course feature Holden, Ford, and Leyland cars built or marketed in Australia, but it also contains a 1946 Allard J1 (Mercury/Ford-engine) of noted competition heritage as a *Candida Provocatores* team car driven by Jim Appleton. MGs are noticeable and Peter Briggs was well known for his MG-based motorsport activities in the 1970s. A 1904 Rover 8hp looks rather odd when set against Australian 'ute' culture, German micro-cars, the 30th oldest VW Beetle known worldwide (1946 dated) and a range of midget racers (midget racers were popular in WA 'desert Grand Prix' races and events further east. Even curiouser is the statement of the 1898 Mercedes 10.5hp single-cylinder that was imported

from the UK as early as 1903. A 1904 Napier adds to the eccentricity! Memorabilia and artefacts are also on show. Local, home-made cake can also be sourced in town. Carnivores will love locally-sourced steak sandwich and a glass of WA Red wine.

Wonderful WA is worth the long flight (try the superb non-stop Qantas QF9/QF10, upon which premium economy is more than comfortable) and the wheatlands east of Perth provide great motoring, the York museum, and for glider enthusiasts, Narrogin Gliding Club where a scenic flight is a must (preferably in their 'DG' glider with the winglets attached). Three are other very good car museums in Western Australia and beyond. See the Australasian Motor Museums Association's website to plan your motoring museum visiting in Australia.

EIRE

KILGARVAN MOTOR MUSEUM

Kilgarvan, Co. Kerry,
Ireland.
Telephone: 064-66-85346
Opening hours: 0930-1245:1345-1730. Tuesday-Saturday. See website for alternative days. November-March, appointments only.
kilgarvanmotormuseum@gmail.com

This is 'different' and good for that. The cars are real in the sense of being original and regularly driven. If you are looking for digital feed and over-restored, shiny plasticised perfection when visiting a museum, then this is not the place for you. But, if true enthusiasm, 'oily rag' philosophy, on-going restoration, and a relaxed atmosphere all appeal, than you should not miss Kilgarvan.

John and Joan Mitchell and their sons have been collecting and restoring vehicles since the mid-1970s as a hobby. During this period, visitors from all over the world have tasted Kilgarvan's unusual offering. Their founding car was an Armstrong-Siddeley Lancaster of 1946.

Porsche, VW Beetle, MG TD, Healey, DKW, American cars, locally built Ford Model T, Vauxhalls, Rolls-Royces, all complement an array of artefacts and 'resto' projects in series of 'sheds'. Several car makers built cars in Ireland – Citroën built a handful of Traction Avants in Dublin. Rarer still are the Adler and Borgward cars that were locally built from imported parts.

Located in the heart of some of the best driving roads in Ireland with stunning scenery to match, Kilgarvan motor museum is close to many of the great driving routes such as the Wild Atlantic Way, the Ring of Kerry, the Ring of Beara as well as some famous rally stages.

Kilgarvan is (thankfully) not 'digital, it is not 'bling', but it is very real, very tangible. In my opinion, it is definitely worth a visit for the dedicated classic car enthusiast, but might not meet wider family, or more modern electronic or 'Pebble Beach' tastes. This place is, after all, about real old cars that work. Hours were spent here and classic car joy found. Kilgarvan is worth heading west for. Highly recommended for the classic, oily rag, or dedicated enthusiast.

FRANCE
LOHÉAC MUSEUM

The Manor of the Automobile and Old Trades of Lohéac
4 Rue de la Cour Neuve – 35550 Loheac,
Brittany,
Tel: 02 99 34 02 32
Museum open daily and on public holidays from 1000 to 1300 and 1400 to 1900 (Closed on Monday).

This truly is one of the best provincial car museums anywhere in the world and offers a true enthusiast experience, yet it is little known in the UK beyond certain car club members and dedicated Francophiles. Just be sure to remember that like many things in rural France, it closes for lunch – a proper long lunch of real food. The museum has its own racing circuit and former and current racing/rally drivers and teams are regular visitors.

Loheac really is a stunning museum where an entire day can be spent marvelling at its myriad contents. It is best to ask for an internal map! Be warned, for its annual auto-jumble and celebration weekend every October everything in the locality is booked out. On one such visit, I ended up sleeping in the only available accommodation – under a hedge – helped by on-site Breton cider and a barbecue.

Situated between Rennes and Redon in Brittany yet just 2½ hours by TGV from Paris and not far from Le Mans (60+ minutes' drive), Loheac offers collection of more than 400 vehicles. If arriving from the Porstmouth-St Malo ferry (on the brilliant, Brittany Ferries of course), simply drive south past Rennes towards Nantes and turn off (west) towards Redon – a total trip of about 95 minutes if the traffic is clear and you can avoid the gendarmes.

Housed in old farm buildings and a purpose built new auditorium, Loheac is a living breathing car shrine that also has an active restoration department, an in-use racing circuit and a simply brilliant annual autojumble (*autobrocante*) and club rally that is the envy of northern France and packed out with campers and visitors who travel from afar for the three-day weekend every October.

The oldest car in the museum is the De Dion Bouton 1899. Also exhibited are examples of the famous 'Taxi of the Marne'; the 1920s are also represented with the Citroën 5HP or Renault NN; post-war cars with the 4CV, Dauphine, 203, Traction, 2CV, Aronde.

Special exhibitions include the 24 Hours of Le Mans. The Museum honours the 24 Hours through famous cars such as the Peugeot 908 HDI FAP or Jaguar XJR11, the Courage Valiant, the Alpine A220, the René Bonnet Aerojet and Panhard DB. Alongside them is one of the two cars enrolled at Le Mans by Michel Hommell in 1994, the Aston Martin DB7.

Of specific motorsport interest is the Group B rally car tribute collection composed of:

1985 Audi Quattro S 1 – 4 RM
1986 Citroen BX 14 TC Evolution
Ford 1986 RS 200 4WD
1984 Lancia 037 Coupe
1985 Lancia Delta S4 – 4 RM
1986 MG Metro 6 R 4
1986 Peugeot 205 T 16 Evolution 2
1986 Renault R 5 Turbo Maxi

Other permanent exhibits include Formula one cars, a large model display, and French marque displays. Key exhibits include:

French cyclecars 1910-1925
Cadillac
Lafayette,
Packard (USA),
Rolls Royce
Jaguar
Mercedes, Tatra Talbot,
Hotchkiss,
Renault
Reinastella,
Panhard and Levassor.
Peugeot
Citroën
Ferrari
Models
Amphibians

Veteran and vintage
Racing cars
Models
Commercial vehicles
Horse drawn devices

There are top quality model and toy displays, a working restoration garage, and the food is of course, superb. This is French enthusiasm at its very best.

From here, I drove many miles east to Michel Pont's wonderful museum at Château de Savigny-les-Beaune, Beaune. This is also a 'must see' and contains aircraft as well as cars, motorcycles and food and wine.

GERMANY

PORSCHE MUSEUM

Porscheplatz 1,
70435 Stuttgart-Zuffenhausen,
Telephone: 00 49 (0)711 - 911 20 911
info.museum@porsche.de
Opening hours: Daily, see website

Is this the ultimate shrine to the automania of a marque? Here in a €100 million emporium, can be found a capturing of the essence of Porsche. Arrayed in a stunning museum lies design, engineering and art all welded together to form a true experience. Like the Saab Museum, it is a one make wonder, but given the make, who is to argue?

The original Porsche museum opened in 1976 in a side-road near the Porsche factory. It was a relatively small 'works' museum with little parking space and it was only big enough to hold around twenty exhibits. Work on the concept for the new Porsche Museum began in 2003. The museum was designed by the architects Delugan Meissl. The exhibition spaces were designed by H.G. Merz, who was also involved in the building of the Mercedes-Benz Museum which is nearby.

The stories of all the iconic Porsches are told here at this museum, and the pre-1939 cars are particularly stunning in their ethos and future-vision. The 911 (901 series) from birth to today is wonderfully chronicled, as are all the Porsches of road and circuit. And suddenly the 944 and 928 seem far more like true Porsches than perceived wisdom has previously allowed. A day here is not enough. Maybe it is best to stay a few days in Stuttgart and see this museum and the Mercedes-Benz Museum too? Oh and why not take a Porsche factory tour as well?

The Porsche Museum truly is the high art of the new museum culture and all its ingredients. There is little one can say other than go if Porsche, or exquisite engineering is your thing. Stunning.

TWO-WHEELS AND NSU MUSEUM

(Deutsches Zweirad und NSU Museum)
Urban Strasse 11
74172 Neckarsulm
Telephone: 07132 35271
Opening hours: 1000-1700 Tuesday to Sunday
www.zweirad-musuem.de

A museum and preserved factory setting, this is of the Neckarsulm Strickmaschine/ Stricken Union – from sewing machines to Neckarsulm Motoren Werke AG or just NSU and it is motorcycle heaven. Shame there is not a bigger Prinz and RO80 hall of fame, but NSU was the world's largest motorcycle manufacture for one brief period of history. A million NSU 'Quickly' mopeds were sold. NSU also built cars prior to the First World War.

Located over several floors in a lovely old building, a former castle it appears, this museum has been open since 1956. 350 motorcycles are on show here, plus NSU cars and artefacts. The 'Zweirad' part is about bicycles and all things two-wheeled, and the NSU part is NSU dedicated. Includes the 1954 NSU Renfox 'Bluwal' racing motorcycle with aero-fairing. Rotary valves, rotary engines, and R. von Koenig Fachsenfeld's aerodynamics work, are all referenced here.

An early 1914 NSU car is on show and there is a Moto Guzzi, and a BMW R51 side car outfit here too. This another brilliant 'non-bling' smaller yet authentic museum that has been reinvented but has not lost its vital ethos and ingredients. A really superb set up, with ancient 'caverns', yet properly done and not over-modernised. Highly recommended for several hours of NSU nostalgia. Cars and motorcycles together, this is a fantastic, 'five-star' museum experience where I spent nearly an entire day. Thank goodness the RO80 was blue!

THE NETHERLANDS
THE LOUWMAN MUSEUM/COLLECTION

Louwman Collection as National Automobile Museum
Steurweg 8, 4941 VR Raamsdonksveer,

Telephone +31 (0)162 58 54 00
Open Tuesday-Sunday (Easter to last Sunday in Oct)
www.louwmancollection.nl

Probably the key collection in Holland, and a private collection at that. Louwman, importer in Holland of Toyota created the largest Toyota collection outside Japan, then added serious classics ranging from a Duesenberg collection, to T50 Bugatti and other Bugatti's. Throw in random classic Alfa Romeos, Ferraris, Maseratis, Lancias, Spykers, Aston Martins and you have a quality collection of international significance. A serious place for the serious enthusiast – who should not miss it.

SWEDEN

SAAB CAR MUSEUM

Åkerssjövägen 18,
SE-461 29 Trollhättan,
Telephone +46 520 289 440
info@saabcarmuseum.se
Opening hours: 1100-1600, days vary: see website.

Set near the falls and weirs of the Gotha canal, amid the delightful town of Trollhattan, and the Gotaland countryside, the Saab Car Museum collection comprises of around 120 cars and approximately 70 of them are on show. All of Saab's aircraft-inspired cars are gathered here in an homage to the Saab car company, itself derived from the the Svenksa Aeroplan Aktie Bolaget (SAAB). Saab in its original Saab aviation company, an entirely separate entity, lived on of course, after the Saab car company died.

Cars, design ideas, prototypes, everything Saab was saved and saved again.

The first car in the museum was the 'flying saucer' of a car that was the UrSaab (Original Saab) 92001 prototype of 1947 – the car the Saab story stemmed from and very much an evocation of an aerofoil on wheels. The Saab Car Museum contains many milestones concerning the 4.4 million Saab cars that have been produced over six decades. Everything from the Swedish welfare state's Saab 92 to the Saab 9-4X and Saab 9-5 prestige vehicles.

The Saab Car Museum first opened its doors in an early incarnation in 1975. The initiator was Albert Trommer, a legendary manager of the activities for visitors at the then Saab-Scania Car division. The first museum premises were old and very modest. Situated in the cellar, under the old Saab-ANA retailer facility,

the museum was not at all easy to find. But everything was there that had been saved and hidden from the scrapyard over the years.

From 1987, the new Saab Museum's opening celebrated the Saab 50th anniversary, as a completely new museum. By the 1990s, after various changes and an interior remodelling of 2005, an incredibly modern 'scandi-design' building emerged as an early star in the new museum sub-culture. Per-Olof 'Pelle' Rudh, who had, been one of the top mechanics at the Saab Competition Department, took over the reins at the museum. Erik Carlsson 'on the roof' was Saab's legendary rally driver, who won the RAC Rally three times in a row, and also the Monte Carlo Rally in 1962-63, and after his active career, worked with public relations at Saab, and his connection with, and involvement in, the museum was always close to his heart. Peter Backstrom became the well-known 'face' of the Saab car museum and today, Saab enthusiasts and Saab club members regularly gather at the museum to both lament and celebrate their beloved Saab. Any car enthusiast would be taken with the museum and its contents. It is a superb museum and resource.

This museum and its staff come very highly recommended and are a compelling example of what enthusiasm and passion for design can achieve. Incredibly modern, obviously part of the new age of museum culture, and yet established many years ago, this is more than a shrine, it is Saabism and something else. Saab's car design and engineering team was always small, and intimate, a true family of 'believers' in an ethos. That tradition shines through at a museum that is not to be missed, even if you are not a Saab follower.

ITALY
DUCATI MUSEUM

Bologna
www.ducati.com
Opening times: 0900 -1800, closed Sunday (also closed Wednesday in winter)

A great selection of Ducati's most famous race bikes and new displays dedicated to the firm's road-going machines. You can sign-up to a factory tour while you are there if you book in advance and if you turn up on a Ducati you can park it in the factory's grounds.

MV AGUSTA MUSEUM

Via Giovanni Agusta,
Malpensa, Milan,
www.museoagusta.it

This museum is in the environs of Milan airport at Malpensa (not Linate) airport but is little known. Comprising of a collection of not only MV's most famous race bikes, but also their helicopters, it charts the firm's history right back to its founding days when Italians made cars, motorcycles and advanced aircraft.

MOTO GUZZI MUSEUM

Via Emanuele, Vittorio Parodi, 23826,
Mandello del Lario, Lecco, Italy.
www.motoguzzi.com/Museum

Located within the historic Moto Guzzi factory at Mandello del Lario, on the picturesque banks of Lake Como in northern Italy, the Museo Moto Guzzi is housed over three floors of the factory building. Contains a collection of over 150 exhibits including all the bikes since 1921, prototypes, race bikes, drawings, memorabilia. A well-worn but true enthusiast museum, and at Lake Como.

USA

MULLIN AUTOMOTIVE MUSEUM

1421 Emerson Avenue,
Oxnard, California, 93033.
Telephone: 805 385 5400
info@mullinautomotivemuseum.com
www.mullinautomotive.com

Superb, stylish, and yes, exquisite, this is the modern private collection as museum taken to the high extremes of funding and personal commitment. Housed in a stunning building created by David R. Hertz, the museum is dedicated to all things Art Deco, Bugatti and a range of other grand marques such as Talbot-Lago, Hispano-Suiza, Delage, Delahaye, all of which are covered, as are 'French Curves'. This very confident museum is something unusual. French and Italian varietals feature, as did a recent tribute to Citroën. The works of a certain G. Voisin (which Mr Mullin struggles to pronounce) are a passion and wonderfully exhibited. Hours of forensic study of carrosserie/carrozzeria and exquisite engineering can be made here.

The displays are superb and the whole experience borders on the ethereal. This is the 'other' world and actually very enjoyable, even if one leaves feeling poor and perhaps excluded from the gilded halls of elitism and the lawns of Monterrey's Pines and Pebble Beach.

Mr Mullin has spent hundreds of millions of his own billions here and we might commend him not only for that philanthropic act, but for the resulting, superb museum experience. But be warned this is not a business class experience, it is way beyond that and is Concours d'Elegance personified – it might even be too perfect – like an over-restored car. Definitely not a place to dress too casual and wander in off the beach. This is a very, very smart, yet authentic and accessible museum that requires you to think, and why not? However, despite the 'bling' it is open to anyone – which is the point.

Semi-private visits to the museum are bookable on Tuesdays at $40. Public entry is on the second and fourth Saturday of each month from 1000-1500 only at lower cost. Be on your best behaviour and if you are not a billionaire, don't worry – after all opinions are only opinions and money is irrelevant to authenticity. Highly Recommended and possibly soon to be replicated in the British countryside at Great Tew.

Meanwhile, the Mullin Automotive Museum in Los Angeles (and also the Petersen Museum which Mullin is associated with), is highly recommended and a 'must see' not least at $15 for a public day ticket. So, *not* elitist at all then.

PETERSEN MUSEUM

6060Wilshire Boulevard,
Los Angeles, California,
www.petersen.org

The world's largest motoring museum, but non-profit as it is an act of philanthropy. Originally founded by Robert E. Petersen and his wife, this museum was spectacularly remodelled into an $125million architectural landmark in recent years.

The museum has 100 vehicles on display across 25 individual galleries. A large store houses cars not on show. A 'Vault' is also on offer at admission charge, and has become a specific feature, no photos allowed down there apparently.

From French carrosserie and Art Deco design through to industrial design, engineering, motorsport, and motorcycles, this collection is certainly eclectic and thought provoking, if a little sterile.

From Porsche to Toyota, via motorcycles, hot rods, sci-fi and film vehicles, French fancies and European fare, the displays are thought provoking and of the highest quality. There is no doubting the Petersen's brilliance, but rather like an over-restored car that has its entire story wiped out in a new-for-old 'bling' rebuild and acrylic respray, the depth of patina and the psychometry of ownership seems missing from the cars and the museum. Has anyone here even looked through the curtain into economy class?

The Petersen is a 'cool' place and recommended but is seemingly aloof, almost too perfect, in my humble opinion. Oh to mess it up a bit and see some 'oily rag' cars. Come on!

SAAB HERITAGE MUSEUM/TOM DONNEY COLLECTION

940 Dickson Drive,
Sturgis,
South Dakota,
SD 57785,
Telephone: (US) 605 720-6399
Opening hours: check website or call
www.saabmuseumusa.com

In a move destined to delight Saab fans, well known Saabist and Bonneville Salt Flats racer, Tom Donney (with wife Patti) has moved the Donney family Saab collection (over 75 cars) to a new 'living' museum Saab heritage collection in Sturgis, South Dakota where car and motorcycle enthusiasts regularly gather. Founded in 2016 and now open, Tom says Saab enthusiasts will also actually be able to drive some of the cars and watch them in a working restoration shop.

The collection includes Donney's own cars and the thirteen examples he purchased from the GM Saab America collection (some of which had been sold to Spyker in 2009). Self-funded and surely deserving of support, this is a fine example of the application of 'new' museum thinking. Highly recommended and don't forget to time your visit to coincide with the motorcycle festival (up to half a million bikers attend) if that appeals.

Also in Sturgis and not to be missed is the Sturgis Motorcycle Museum, which lays a vital role in the annual Sturgis motorcycle festival.

STURGIS MOTORCYCLE MUSEUM & HALL OF FAME

99 Main Street,
Sturgis, South Dakota,
SD 57785.
Opening hours: 0900-1700 Seven days a week

USA Quick Reference Guide (see below for full guide)
A quick reference guide to notable American motor museums:

America's Car Museum Tacoma Washington State.
Antique Automobile Club of America, Hershey Penn.
Barber Vintage Motorsports Museum, Leeds, Alabama.
Collier Collection Naples, Florida.
The Henry Ford Museum Dearborn Michigan.
Indianapolis Motor Speedway Hall of Fame Indiana.
Lane Motor Museum Nashville Tennesse.
Larsz Anderson Auto Museum Brookline Massachusetts.
Mullin Automotive Museum Oxnard CA.
Mungenast Classic Motorcycle Museum, Saint Louis Missouri
National Automobile Museum, Reno Nevada.
National Corvette, Museum Bowling Green, Kentucky.
Petersen Automotive Museum Los Angeles CA.
Revs Institiute Naples, Florida.
Simeone Foundation Automotive Museum, Philadelphia, Pennsylvania.

GLOBAL MOTOR MUSEUMS DIRECTORY

(Note: Some museums may not be open at date of publication)

Abu Dhabi
Emirates National Auto Museum, Abu Dhabi, United Arab Emirates
Al Ain Classic Car Museum

Andorra
National Automobile Museum

Argentina
Automovil Club Argention A.C.A., Buenos Aires
Museo Juan Manuel Fangio, Balcarce

Australia
Antique Motorcycles, Victoria
Ash's Speedway Museum New South Wales
Australian Motorlife/Butler Collection, Woolongong, New South Wales
Baillup Ford Fram Museum, West Australia

Ballart Collection, Victoria
Bichneo Motorcycle Museum, Tasmania
Carl Lindner Jaguar Collection, South Australia
Campes Motor Museum, Victoria
Charlies Motor Museum, Victoria
Coleraine Classic Cars
Fox Collection, Victoria,
Geelong Collection of Motoring, Victoria
Goolwah Motor Museum, South Australia
Gunnedah Rural Museum, New South Wales
Gosford Classic Car Museum
Gippsland Vehicle Collection, Victoria
Indian Motorcycle Museum of Australia, Virginia, Queensland
Lost in the 50s, New South Wales
McFeeters Motors, New South Wales
Mildura Holden Museum, Victoria
Morris Minor Garage, Victoria
Motorcycle Australia Museum, Victoria
Motorist Collection, Victoria
Motorlife Museum, New South Wales
Motor Museum of Western Australia
National Automobile Museum of Tasmania
National Holden Museum, Victoria
National Motor Museum, South Australia
National Motor Racing Museum at Mount Panorama, New South Wales
National Military Vehicle Museum, South Australia
National Motorcycle Museum, Nabiac, New South Wales
National Transport Museum New South Wales
Nuthouse Motor Collection, West Australia
Panorma Motorcycle Museum, Brisbane, Queensland
Peterborough Motorcycle Museum, South Australia
Phillip Island History of Motorsport, Victoria
Powerhouse Motorcycle Museum, Tamworth, New South Wales
RACV Collection, Queensland
Richardsons Harley Davidson and Buell Museum, Launceston, Tasmania
Ridley Motor Museum, West Australia
Shepparton Motor Museum, Victoria
Sir Henry Royce Foundation Victoria
Stein Motorcycle Museum, Mudgee New South Wales
Tractor Museum, West Australia
Trafalgar Holden Museum, Victoria
Transport and Heritage Centre, Queensland

Trevan Collection, New South Wales
Qantas Founders Museum, Queensland
Queensland Motorsport Museum, Queensland
West Coast Motor Museum, West Australia
Westbury Steam Museum, Tasmania
Wonders of Wynyard
York Motor Museum/Avon Valley Motor Museum, West Australia
4C's Motor Museum, Victoria

Austria
Automobil Museum Aspang

Barbados
Mallalieu Motor Collection, Hastings, Bridgetown

Belgium
Autoworld
Mahymobiles
Abarth Works Guy Moerenhout Racing
Old Timer Museum/Vintage Motorcycle Museum

Brazil
Museu do Automóvel de Sau Paulo
Museu do Automóvel de Ceará
Museu do Automóvel de Curitiba
Museu do Automóvel Arte & Historia

Bulgaria
Retro-Museum,Varna

Canada
Canadian Automotive Museum
Manitoba Antique Automobile Museum
Assiniboia Museum, Assiniboia, Saskatchewan
Western Development Museum, Moose Jaw, Saskatchewan

Cayman Islands
Cayman Motor Museum

Chile
Auto Museum Moncopulli, Puyehue

Jedimar Car Museum, Santiago
Salon Antique Car Museum, Quilicura
Santa Cruz Auto Museum, Santa Cruz

China
Grand Prix Museum, Macau, China
Beijing Classic Car Museum
Beijing Auto Museum
Chancun International Auto Park
Classic Auto Cycle Museum Hong Kong
FAW Collection
Grand Prix Museum, Macau
Luo Wenyou Classic Car Museum
Nanjing Auto Museum
SAIC Museum
Shanghai Auto Museum

Croatia
Ferdinand Budicki Automobile Museum

Cuba
Havana Car Museum

Cyprus
Cyprus Historic & Classic Motor Museum

Czech Republic
Škoda Auto Museum, Mladá Boleslav
Tatra Technology Museum, Kopřivnice
National Technical Museum, Prague
Veteran Car/ Motor Museum, Znojmo
Note* Other provincial Czech auto museums exist

Denmark
Jytlandic Automobile Museum
Sommer's Automobile Museum
Danish Museum of Science & technology
Stojer Samlingen

Egypt
Ezzat Collection, Zamalek, Cairo

Eire (Ireland)
Kilgarvin Motor Museum
Transport Museum of Ireland

Estonia
Automuseum, Halinga
Cafe Museum, Tallin
MOMU/Motor Sport Museum of Estonia
Museum of Soviet Vehicles, Jarva-Jaani

Finland
Mobilia, Kangasala
The Car Museum of Vehoniemi
Uudenkaupungin Automuseo
Oulun Automuseo
Espoon Automuseo

France
Château de Savigny-les-Beaune, Beaune
Château de Sanxet, Pomport
Conservatoire de l' Agricole, Chartres
Conservatoire Citroën, Paris
Conservatoire de la Monoplace, Circuit Nevers Magny Cours
Fondation Berliet, Lyons
L'Espace Museum Automobiles Matra, Romoratin-Lantheny
Loheac Museum (Musee de la Manoir Loheac), Rennes
Lorraine Motor Museum
Musée National de l'Automobile (Cité de l'Automobile), Schlumph Collection, Mulhouse
Musée de l'Aventure Peugeot, Sochaux
Musée Charoliais du Mechanism Agricole, Salviac
Musée Maurice Dufresne, Azay-le-Rideau
Musée du Machinisme de Agricole et Automobile de Salviac, Cahors
Musée de Mecanique Naturelle, Giverny
Musée Regional du Machanism Agricole, La Ferte Milon
Musée des 24 Heures du Mans
Musée National de la Voiture et du Tourisme, Château de Compiègne
Musée Automobile, Reims
Renault Museum, Paris

Germany

Audi Forum, Neckarsulm, and Audi/August Horch Museum, Zwickau
Autostadt, Wolfsburg
Automobile Welt, Eisenach
Automuseum Dr. Carl Benz
Autosammlung, Steim
Autostadt (VW)
BMW Museum, Munich
Classic Remise, Berlin, Dusseldorf
Maybach Museum
Mercedes-Benz Museum, Stuttgart
Museum Autovision
Museum for Historical Maybach
Museum Mobile (Audi)
NSU/Two Wheel Museum, Neckarsulm
Opel Museum, Russselsheim
Opel Museum, Herne
Porsche Museum, Stuttgart
Sinsheim Auto & Technik Museum
Technikmuseum Speyer
Prototyp – Personen KraftWagen, Hamburg
EFA-Museum für Deutsche Automobilgeschichte
Westerwald Museum

Georgia

Tbilisi Auto Museum

Greece

Hellenic Motor Museum

India

Ashvok Vintage Museum, Nivem
B.E.S.T. Bus Museum, Mumbai
Car Manjusha, Dharmasthala
Dungarpur Motor Museum, Dungarpur
G.D. Naidu Museum, Coimbatore
GeeDee Car Museum, Tamil Nadu
Heritage Motor Museum, Gurgaon
Mini Classic Museum, Ooty
Pranlal Bhogilal Vintage Auto Museum, Ahmedabad

Subhash Sanas Vintage Museum
Sudha Cars Museum
Vintage Museum Udaipur Palace, Udaipur

Indonesia
Museum Angkut, Batu

Iran
National Car Museum of Iran, Tehran

Israel
Tefen Car Collection, Tefen
Ralex Automobile Museum, Ashdod

Italy
Agusta (MV Augusta) Museum
Centro Storico Fiat / FCA Heritage
Ducati Museum
Moto Guzzi Museum
Museo Ferrari
Museo Nazionale dell'Automobile
Museo Casa Enzo Ferrari
Museo Ferruccio Lamborghini
Museo Lamborghini
Museo Nazionale dell' Automobile
Museo Storico Alfa Romeo
Museo Mille Miglia
Museo Vincenzo Lancia
Museo Lancia
Museo Targa Florio
Museo Nicolis
Piaggio Museum
Pininfarina Museum

Japan
Toyota Automobile Museum
Toyota Mega Web
Historic Car Gallery, Dachi
Honda Collection Hall, Motegi, Tochigi
Humobility World (Daihatsu), Ikeda, Osaka
Maehara 20th Kiryū, Gunma
Matsuda Collection (Mazda)

Mazda Museum, Hiroshima
Mitsubishi Auto Gallery, Okazaki, Aichi
Motorcar Museum of Japan, Komatsu, Ishikawa
Museo della Cinquecento (Japan), Tsuruoka, Yamagata
Nissan Engine Museum, Yokohama
Nissan Heritage Collection, Zama, Kanagawa
Prince & Skyline Museum, Okaya, Nagano
Shikoku Motor Car Museum, Kōnan, Kōchi
Suzuki Plaza, Hamamatsu, Shizuoka
Toyota Automobile Museum, Nagakute, Aichi
Toyota Commemorative Museum of Industry and Technology, Nagoya, Aichi
Toyota Kuragaike Commemorative Hall, Toyota, Aichi
Yamaha Communication Plaza, Yamaha, Iwata, Shizuoka
Wakui Museum, Kazo, Saitama

Kuwait
Historical Vintage, and Classical Cars Museum

Latvia
Riga Motor Museum, Riga

Malaysia
National Automobile Museum, Sepang

Malta
Malta Classic Car Museum

Mexico
Mexico Automobile Museum, Mexico City
Puebla Automobile Museum, Mexico City
Monterrery Museum, Monterrey

Monaco
Monaco Top Cars Collection, Fontvieille

Morocco
Morocco National Classical Auto Museum, Temara
Morocco National 4x4 Museum, Merzouga

Netherlands
American Motorcycle Museum Holland, Raalte
Automuseum Bergeyk

Brandweer (Fire service/fire engine) Museum, Borculo
DAF Museum, Eindhoven
Haag's Openbaar Vervoer Museum (M. of Public Transportation) S'Gravenhage
Hartog's Ford Museum, Hillegom
Histo Mobil, Giethoorn
Louwman Collection Nationaal Automobile-Museum, Raamsdonksveer
Opel Museum, Tijne
Openbaar Vervoer Museum (Ministry of Public Transportation) Borculo
Massey-Harris-Ferguson MHF Museum, Schagen
Museum 1939-1945, Uithuizen
Nationaal Brandweermuseum, Hellevoetsluis
Nationaal Ambulance-en-Eerstehulpmuseum, Apeldoorn
Noordelijk Busmuseum, Winschoten
Velorama National Bicycle Museum, Nijmegen
Oldtimermuseum De Rijke, Oostvoorne
Rijksmuseum Paleis Het Loo, Apeldoorn

New Zealand
Bill Richardson Transport World
Museum of Transport and Technology
National Transport and Toy Museum
Nelson Classic Car Collection
Omaka Classic Cars
Southward Car Museum
Warbirds and Wheels
Yaldhurst Museum

Norway
Norsk Motorhistorisk Museum
Norweigian Vehicle Museum
Norweigian Road Museum
Veteran Car Museum Geiranger
Horton Automobile Museum

Pakistan
National Museum

Paraguay
Several private collections are planned to open.

Peru
Asociacion Museo Del Automovil, La Molina
Museo de Autos Antiguous Coleccion Nicolini

Poland
Automotive and Technology Museum, Warsaw
Muzeum Mtoroyzacji Gydnskie
Muzeum Inżynierii Miejskiej w Krakowie, Krakow

Portugal
Ancient Auto Museum
Carris Museum, Lisbon
Famalicao Automobile Museum, Oporto
Miniature Car Museum, Gouveia
Museu do Automovel, Ribeirao
Museu do Caramulo, Caramulo
Museo Nacional des Cohes, Belem
SportClasse Porsche Collection, Lisbon

Romania
Tiriac Collection, Bucharest

Russia
AvtoVAZ Museum, (Lada), Tolyatti
Retro Auto museum, Moscow
Lomakov's old-timers cars and motorcycles Museum, Moscow
Autoville, Moscow
First Private Museum of Retro and Military Vehicles, Moscow
Vintage Cars Museum, Saint Petersburg
Retro Cars Museum, Vyborg
Retro Cars Museum, Zelenogorsk
Retro Cars Museum, Yekaterinburg
UMMC Auto Museum, Verkhnyaya Pyshma, Yekaterinburg

San Marino
Maranello Rosso Museum

Serbia
Muzej Automobila, Belgrade

Singapore
National Tram Museum
Land Transport Gallery

Slovakia
Veteran Car Museum, Bratislava

South Africa
Auto Pavillion VW
Franschhoek Motor Museum
Datsun Heritage Museum, Rosslyn
James Hall Transport Museum, Johannesburg
Rupert Museum, Stellenbosch
Wijnland Auto Museum, Capetown
Note* Several private collections also exist in SA

South Korea
Samsung Transport Museum
Renault Samsung Motors Gallery
Hyundai Kia R&D Museum
Samsung Transportation Museum
Hyundai Motor, Seoul

Spain
Museo Automovilístico de Málaga
Museo de Historia de la Automoción de Salamanca
Museo de Coches Clásicos y Antiguos Torre Loizaga, Galdames

Sweden
Göran Karlsson's Motor Museum, Ullared
Johannamuseet, Skane
Marcus Wallenberg Museum Hall (Scania/Vabis/Saab)
Motala Motor Museum, Motala
Saab Car Museum, Trollhattan
Swedish Opel Museum
Volvo Museum, Gothenburg

Switzerland
Autobau Museum, Romanshorn
Emil Fey Classics Museum, Safenwil
Fondation Pierre Gianadda, Martigny

Monterverdi Museum, Binningen
Pantheon Museum, Basel
Swiss Transport Museum, Zurich
Vintage Car Museum, Leman
Transport Museum Lucerne

Thailand
Jesada Transport Museum, Bangkok

Turkey
Key Classic Car Museum, Torbal, Izmir
Rahmi M. Koç Museum, Hasköy, Istanbul
Sabri Artam Classic Car Museum, Çengelköy, Istanbul
Tofaş Museum of Cars and Anatolian Carriages, Bursa
Ural Ataman Classic Car Museum, Tarabya, Istanbul

Ukraine
AvtoZAZ Museum, Zaporizhia

USA
Academy of Art University Automobile Museum,San Francisco, California
Allen Unique Autos, Grand Junction, Colorado
American Classic Motorcycle Museum, Asheboro, North Carolina
America's Car Museum, Tacoma, Washington
American Motorcycle Association Motorcycle Hall of Fame, Ohio
America On Wheels, Allentown, Pennsylvania
AACA Museum, Hershey, Pennsylvania
America on Wheels, Allentown, Pennsylvania
America's Packard Museum, Dayton, Ohio
Antique Car Museum of Iowa, Coralville, Indiana
Auburn Cord Duesenberg Automobile Museum, Auburn, Indiana
Antique Motorcycle Club of America Gallery, Hershey, Pennsylvania
Auto Collections, Imperial Palace, Las Vegas, Nevada
Automobile Driving Museum, El Segundo, California
Barber Vintage Motorsports Museum, Birmingham, Alabama
Beller Museum, Romeoville, Illinois
Bill's Old Bike Barn, Pennsylvania
Blackhawk Automotive Museum, Danville, California
Bluegrass Motorcycle Museum, Hartford, Kentucky
Buddy Stubbs Harley-Davidson Collection, Phoenix, Arizona
Buffalo Transportation Pierce-Arrow Museum, Buffalo, New York

California Automobile Museum, Sacramento, California
Champlain Valley Transportation Museum, Plattsburg, New York
Canton Classic Car Museum, Canton, Ohio
City Garage Car Museum, Greeneville, Tennesse
Classic Car Collection, Kearney,
Cole Land Transportation Museum, Bangor, Maine
Cooley Museum, San Diego, California
Crawford Auto-Aviation Museum, Cleveland, Ohio
Cussler Museum, Arvada, Colorado
Cycle-Moore Collection Interlochen, Michigan
Dan Roult Museum, Colovis, Claiforina
Deluxe Vintage Motorcycle Museum, Gillette Wyoming
Dick's Classic Garage Car Museum, San Marcos, Texas
Doughertey Museum Collection, Longmont, Colorado
Dream Car Museum, Evansville, Indiana
Ford Piquette Avenue Plant, Detroit, Michigan
Forney Museum, Denver, Colorado
Fort Lauderdale Antique Car Museum, Fort Lauderdale
Fountainhead Antique Auto Museum, Fairbanks, Alaska
Four States Auto Museum, Texarkana, Arkansas
Frick Car & Carriage Museum, Pittsburgh, Pennsylvania
Garlits (don) Museum of Drag Racing, Ocala, Florida
Glenn H. Curtiss Museum, Hammondsport, New York
Gilmore Car Museum, Hickory Corners, Michigan
GM Heritage Center, Sterling Heights, Michigan
Harley Davidson Museum, Milwaukee, Wisconsin
Harley Drag Racing (Legends) Museum (Ray Price), Raleigh, North Carolina
Haas Museum, / Motorcycle Gallery, Dallas, Texas
Hemken Collection, Williams, Indiana
Henry Museum (Ford Motor Company), Dearborn, Michigan
Hill Country Motorcycle Museum, Burnet, Texas
Hostetler's Hudson Auto Museum, Shipshewana, Indiana
Hugh's Bultaco Museum, Craryville, New York
Fort Lauderdale Antique Car Museum, Fort Lauderdale, Florida
Fountainhead Antique Auto Museum, Fairbanks, Alaska
Frick Car & Carriage Museum, Pittsburgh, Pennsylvania
Indianapolis Motor Speedway Hall of Fame Museum, Speedway, Indiana
Kaiser Bill's Collection, Altonah, Utah
Kansas City Automotive Museum, Olathe, Kansas
Kimball-Browning Collection, Ogden, Utah
Kokomo Automotive Museum, Kokomo, Indiana

Lake Hill Motorcycle Museum, Michigan
Lane Motor Museum, Nashville, Tennessee
Larz Anderson Auto Museum, Brookline, Massachusetts
Laughlin Classic Car Collection, Laughlin, Nevada
LeMay Family Collection, Tacoma, Washington
Logue (Bob) Motorsports Honda Museum, Williamsport, Pennsylvania
Lone Star Motorcycle Museum, Vanderpool, Texas
Lynden Power Museum, Lynden, Washington
Marconi Automotive Museum, Tustin, California
Martin Auto Museum, Phoenix, Arizona
Melvin Motorcycle Museum, Oscoda, Michigan
Memory Lane Motorsports & Historic Auto Museum, Mooresville, North Carolina
Miami Auto Museum / Dezer Collection, North Miami
Miles Through Time Automotive Museum, Toccoa, Georgia
Montana Auto Musuem, Deer Lodge, Montana
Montz Motocycle Museum, Tecumseh, Nebrasaka
Motodoffo Vintage Collection, Temecula, California
Motocross Early Years Museum, Villa Park, California
Motorcycle Hall of Fame, Pickering, Ohio
Motorcyclepedia, Newburgh, New York
Motorcycle Museum and Cafe, Grove, Oklahoma
Motorsport Hall of Fame, Novi, Michigan
Moto Talbot Motorocycle Museum, Carmel, California
Mullin Automotive Museum, Oxnard, California
Mungenast Classic Motorcycle Museum, Saint Louis Missouri
Murphy Auto Museum, Oxnard, California
Museum of Automobiles, Morrilton, Arizona
Museum of Alaska Transportation and Industry, Wasilla, Alaska
Museum of Automobiles, Morrilton, Arkansas
Muscle Car City, Punta Gorda, Florida
National Automotive & Truck Museum, Auburn, Indiana
National Corvette Museum, Bowling Green, Kentucky
National Packard Museum, Warren, Ohio
National Automobile Museum/ Harrah collection, Reno, Nevada
Nethercutt Collection, Sylmar California
New England Motorcycle Museum, Vernon, Connecticut
Newport Car Museum, Newport, Rhode Island
Northeast Classic Car Museum, Norwich, New York
Northwest Vintage Car and Motorcycle Museum Salem, Oregon
National Auto Museum, Loudon, New Hampshire
National Motorcycle Museum, Ananosa, Iowa

National Packard Museum, Warren, Ohio
Newburgh Motorcycle Museum, New York
Nostalgia Street Rods, Goldstrom's Automobile Collection, Las Vegas, Nevada
Old Spokes Auto Museum, New Smithville, Pennsylvania
Owls Head Transportation Museum, Owls Head, Maine
Pacific Northwest Museum of Motorcycling, Seattle, Washington
Penske Racing Museum, Scottsdale, Arizona
Petersen Automotive Museum, Los Angeles, California
Pioneer Village, Minden, Nebraska
Pontiac-Oakland Museum & Resource Center, Pontiac, Illinois
R. E. Olds Transportation Museum, Lansing, Michigan
Revs Institute Naples, Florida
Reynolds-Alberta Museum, Elkhorn, Manitoba
Rocky Mountain Motorcycle Museum, Colarado Springs, Colorado
Route 66 Vintage Iron, Miami, Oklahoma
Saab Heritage Museum/TomDonney Collection, Sturgis, South Dakota
San Diego Automotive Museum, San Diego, California
Sarasota Classic Car Museum, Florida
Saratoga Automobile Museum, Saratoga Springs, New York
Seal Cove Auto Museum, Seal Cove, Maine
Shelby American Collection, Boulder, Colorado
Simeone Foundation Automotive Museum, Philadelphia, Pennsylvania
Solvang Vintage Motorcycle Museum, Solvang, California
South Dakota Auto Museum, Murdo, South Dakota
South Texas Motorcycle Museum, Edinburg, Texas
Speedway Motors Museum of American Speed, Lincoln, Nebraska
Springfield Indian Museum, Massachusetts
Stahls Automotive Foundation, Chesterfield, Michigan
St Francis Motorcycle Museum, Kansas
Studebaker National Museum, South Bend, Indiana
Sturgis Motorcycle Museum, Sturgis, South Dakota
Talladega International Motorsports Hall of Fame, Alabama
Tallahassee Automotive Museum, Tallahassee, Florida
Tampa Bay Automobile Museum, Pinellas Park, Florida
Tired Iron Museum, Cuylerville, New York State
Toyota USA Automobile Museum Torrance, California
Tupelo Automobile Museum, Tupelo, Mississippi
Twisted Oz Motorcycle Museum, Augusta, Kansas
Unique Antique Auto Museum, Marmath, North Dakota
Unser Racing Museum, Alburguerque, New Mexico
Vintage Motorcycle Museum, Chehalas, Washington

Vintage Spokes Museum, Rockford, Illinois
Vintage Tracks, Bloomfield, New York
Volo Museum, Volo Illinois
Western Antique Aeroplane & Automobile Museum, Hood River, Oregon
Wheels Museum, Albuquerque, New Mexico
Wheels O' Time Museum, Peoria, Illinois
Wheels Through Time Motorcycle Musuem, Maggie, North Carolina
William E. Swigart, Jr. Antique Automobile Museum, Huntingdon, Pennsylvania
Wills Sainte Claire Auto Museum, Marysville, Michigan
Wisconsin Automotive Museum, Hartford, Wisconsin
Woodland Auto Display, Paso Robles, California
World of Speed, Wilsonville, Oregon
Motor Museum, Boise, Idaho
Ypsilanti Auto Heritage Museum, Ypsilanti, Michigan

Uruguay
Eduardo Iglesias Automobile Museum, Montevideo
Museo del Automovil, Montevideo

UK
Aerospace Bristol
Amberley Museum & Heritage Centre
Anglesey Transport Museum
Anson Engine Museum
Atwell-Wilson Museum
Aston Martin Heritage Trust
Battlesbridge Motorcycle Museum
Beamish Museum
Bentley (W.O.) Memorial Foundation
Bentley Wildfowl and Motor Museum
Betws-Y-Coed Motor Museum
Bexhill Museum
Bicester Heritage
Biggar Albion Foundation
Birmingham Science Museum 'Thinktank'
Bo'ness Motor Museum
British Commercial Vehicle Museum
British Motor Museum
Brooklands Museum
Bubble Car Museum
Bugatti Trust

Caister Castle Museum
Canvey Island Transport Museum
Clark (Jim) Museum
Cloverlands Model Car Museum
Craven Motorcycle Museum
Crich Tramway Museum
Cotswold Motoring Museum and Toy Collection
Coventry Transport Museum
David Brown Tractor Collection
David Coulthard Museum
David Silver Honda Collection
Design Museum London
Dundee Transport Museum
Dunsfold Collection
Ferguson Family Museum
Filching Manor Motor Museum
Ford Heritage Centre
Glenluce Motor Museum
Gloucester Museum & Archives/ Gloucester heritage
Grampian Transport Museum
Haynes International Motor Museum
History on Wheels Museum
Ipswich Transport Museum
Isle of Man Motor Museum/Cunningham Collection
Jurby Transport Museum
Lakeland Motor Museum
Lanchester Museum & Library
Llangollen Motor Museum
Lincolnshire Road Transport Museum
London Bus Preservation Trust (Museum)
London Motorcycle Museum
Maldon Museum of Power
Manx Transport Heritage Motor Museum
Milestones Museum
Moray Motor Museum
Murrays Motorcycle Museum
Museum of Lincolnshire Life
Museum of Liverpool (Transport)
Museum of Manchester (Transport)
Myreton Motor Museum
National Motor Museum

National Motorcycle Museum
National Museum Cardiff
National Trust Carriage Museum
Northwest Museum of Road Transport
North Yorkshire Motor Museum (Matthewsons)
Oakham Treasures Tractor & Farm Museum (Bristol)
On Your Marques
Oxford Bus Museum and Morris Motors Museum
Pallot Steam, Motor & General Museum
Patrick Collection
Riverside Museum of Transport
Royal Electrical and Mechanical Engineers (REME) Museum
Sammy Miller Museum
Scaleby Hill Vintage Motorcycle Museum/Mike Barry Museum
Science Museum (The) & Wroughton Store/ Science/Museum Group
Scottish Vintage Bus Museum
Shuttleworth Collection
Stanford Hall Museum
Streetlife Museum of Transport
Stonehurst Farm Motor Museum
Studio434
Swansea Bus Museum
Ulster Transport Museum
Williams F1/Heritage Museum
Whitewebbs Museum of Transport
Wirral Transport Museum & Heritage Tramway

Vietnam
HeriTran Classic Car Museum, Hanoi
Ho Chi Minh City Museum Car Collection

BIBLIOGRAPHY

The Author's own published and unpublished works.

Beattie, Ian, *The Complete book of Automobile Body Design*, Haynes, Sparkford, 1977.

Black, Graham. *The Engaging Museum.* Routledge, Oxford 2005.

Hart, Anna, MA *Museum Studies*, Thesis 2008.

Hein, George, E. *Learning in the Museum.* Routledge, Oxford 1998.

Hooper-Greenhill, Eilean, *The Educational role of the Museum.* Leicester Readers in Museum Studies. Routledge Oxford 1994-2005.

Scott-Moncrieff, D. *Veteran and Edwardian Motor Cars.* Batsford Ltd, London 1955.

Stobbs, William, *Motor Museums of Europe.* Arthur Baker Ltd. London 1983.

Periodicals
Bugantics Bugatti Owners Club
Classic Bikes Bauer Media
Classic and Sports Car. Haymarket Publishing. London
Octane. Dennis Publishing. London
Classic Cars. Bauer Media. Peterborough
Practical Classics Bauer Media
Classic Car Weekly Bauer Media
Sports & Exotic Car (Hemmings USA)
Selected Museum Guides and their on-line resources

C000063885